ERRATA.

Page 6, line 11, *for* " James II." *read* " Charles II."
Page 40, line 37, *for* " last " *read* " least."
Page 56, Footnote, *for* " Caven " *read* " Cavan."
Page 68, line 20, *for* " Germany " *read* " German."
Page 74, line 3, *for* " Society " *read* " Soviet."

Reproduced by permission of the artist, M. de Lazlo, and the publishers.

Field Marshal The Right Hon.
The Earl Roberts of Kandahar and Pretoria & of the City of Waterford,
V.C., K.G., K.P., P.C., G.C.B., O.M., G.C.S.I., G.C.I.E.,
Colonel The Irish Guards. Oct. 17th, 1900, until Nov. 14th, 1914.

A Short History
OF THE
Irish Guards

Colonel-in-Chief:
HIS MAJESTY KING GEORGE V.

The Colonel of the Regiment:
GENERAL THE EARL OF CAVAN,
K.P., G.C.B., G.C.M.G., G.C.V.O., G.B.E.

The Lt.-Colonel Commanding the Regiment:
COLONEL R. V. POLLOK,
C.B.E., D.S.O.

PRICE **1/-.**

Printed by
Benham and Company, Ltd., Colchester.
1931.

CONTENTS.

PREFATORY NOTE.

The object of the Army Authorities in prescribing the study of Regimental History, as part of the syllabus for Second and Third Class Certificates of Education, and for Non-Commissioned Officers' Promotion Examinations, was no doubt primarily intended to foster the spirit of the Regiment.

It is, however, impossible to study the history of any of the older regiments without gaining considerable knowledge of the history of England.

In the case of the Irish Guards, who were only formed in 1900, *this is not possible.*

In order to give this short history a wider scope, chapters have been included on the history of the Irish Regiments, to commemorate whose gallantry in the South African War the Irish Guards were formed ; and also the history of the Brigade of Guards, of which the Regiment has the honour to form part.

By the inclusion of these two chapters almost the whole history of the wars of England, except those fought in India, is touched upon.

However great the services rendered by any particular Regiment in a campaign may be, those services are very small compared to the effort made by the Army as a whole.

This short history of the Irish Guards has been compiled by Lieutenant T. H. H. Grayson, in the hope that it will enable the reader to acquire some knowledge of the history of the Irish Guards, and the relationship which that history bears to the history of the British Army and the Brigade of Guards.

R. V. POLLOK, Colonel.
Lieut.-Colonel Commanding Irish Guards.

Regimental Headquarters,
Birdcage Walk, S.W.
July, 1931.

INTRODUCTION.

"Her Majesty the Queen having deemed it desirable to commemorate the bravery shown by the Irish Regiments during the operations in South Africa in the years 1899–1900 has been graciously pleased that an Irish Regiment of Foot Guards be formed, to be designated the 'Irish Guards.'" Army Order, dated, April 7, 1900.

The above quoted Army Order was the first intimation received of Her Majesty's intention to raise an Irish Regiment of Foot Guards.

It is held by many that an Irish Regiment of Guards had been formed in Ireland by James II. in 1662, and that Queen Victoria, in taking this step, was only reviving the regiment. The Regiment of Irish Guards which was formed by Queen Victoria claims no connection with any other regiment of the past. As a matter of interest, the history of the Duke of Ormond's regiment is given later.

At the Restoration, in 1660, when Charles II. returned to the throne, he proceeded to copy the system in vogue at the Continental courts and established a bodyguard. This body-guard, or regiment of foot-guards, subsequently became the Grenadier and Coldstream Guards.

The Duke of Ormond, who was made Viceroy of Ireland, desiring to copy his Royal Master, obtained a commission from Charles II. on April 23rd, 1662, to raise a Regiment of Guards for service *in* Ireland. This regiment was raised and recruited entirely in England and was then transported to Dublin, arriving on May 28th. The regiment is variously alluded to in contemporary correspondence as "The King's Regiment of Foot," "His Majesty's Regiment of Guards *for* Ireland," but never as the Irish Guards. The regiment was quartered in Dublin. In 1666 this regiment helped to suppress a serious mutiny at Carrickfergus in Ireland, and took part in the Dutch Wars of 1673, serving as marines.

On the accession of James II, when Clarendon was Viceroy of Ireland, the original composition of the Guards *in* Ireland began to change and at this period the Regiment in composition must have been very like the Irish Guards as we know them. James II. determined to get rid of all the Protestants from his service, and in 1685 he sent Tyrconnel to Ireland to carry out the changes. Tyrconnel was appointed Lieutenant-General of the Army in Ireland and proceeded to turn out most of the Officers of the Regiment of Guards and to discharge 500 men.

A young Englishman, Sir William Dorrington, who subsequently proved himself to be a very fine soldier, was appointed to command, and he proceeded to try and recruit the Regiment up to strength by enlisting Irishmen from Connaught. This is the first mention of any Irishmen being recruited for the Regiment, and it is recorded that the regiment was never up to strength.

In 1688 William landed in England and seized the throne. The Regiment of Guards in Ireland remained true to James II., and under the command of Dorrington fought at the siege of Derry, the battles of Aughrim and Boyne, and finally surrendered at Limerick. Five hundred of those who surrendered elected to go into exile and formed the nucleus of the Irish Brigade which took service under the King of France and afterwards gained a great reputation on the Continent.

The regiment of Guards in Ireland was finally struck off the roll of the British Army in 1690.

It will be seen from the above, therefore, that the regiment of Guards in Ireland was an English regiment which served in Ireland, and it was only from 1685–1688 that it had any Irishmen in it. From 1688–1690 the regiment, while remaining true to James II., was, as far as England was concerned, a rebel regiment.

The history of the Brigade of Guards dates back to the Restoration of Charles II. in 1660. The Grenadier, Coldstream and Scots Guards are therefore amongst the most ancient regiments in the British Army; they were famous fighting regiments more than a hundred years before many other regiments were raised or thought of.

In every quarter of the globe where British soldiers have fought, with the sole exception of India, and in every great war, the Brigade of Guards has borne its part, and the names of the many famous campaigns and victories emblazoned on the Colours bear witness to its former services.

No soldiers have greater cause for pride than those of the Brigade of Guards. It has been, and still is, the privilege of a regiment of the Brigade of Guards to guard the Sovereign in times of peace and war. This is the reason that so much is expected of the Brigade, and it should set to all other regiments an example of efficiency, smartness and good behaviour.

The motto of the Brigade of Guards is "Tria Juncta in uno" ("Three joined in one"). This motto was chosen when there were only the three regiments, the Grenadiers, Coldstream and Scots Guards. Now, as we know, there are five regiments,* but the motto has remained the same, as has also the spirit of it, in which the members of the five regiments are united as one great regiment—the "Brigade of Guards."

* The Welsh Guards were formed on February 27th, 1915.

CHAPTER I.

The History of the Brigade.

In order to understand the origin of the regiments which compose the Brigade of Guards, it is necessary to know something of the conditions which prevailed in England prior to 1660. Shortly they were as follows :—

King Charles I., who came to the throne in 1625, soon found himself involved in quarrels with his Parliament. Into the reasons for these quarrels we need not enter ; it is sufficient for our purpose, that in 1642 they culminated in civil war between the King and his supporters on the one side, and Parliament and its supporters on the other.

Both parties at once set themselves the task of raising armies, for it must be remembered that in those days there was no regular army such as we have to-day. If troops were needed for any particular purpose they were raised and then disbanded as soon as their work was over.

In these circumstances it is not surprising that the armies that each side raised were entirely ill-disciplined and ill-trained. The year 1643, however, saw the rise on the Parliamentary side of a really great leader. His name was Oliver Cromwell. He was the first man to realise that without discipline and training an army can achieve nothing, and that disciplined troops will always defeat undisciplined troops in the long run. He set himself first of all to train and discipline his own regiment. So successful was he that Parliament, in 1645, authorized the raising of a new army to be trained according to Cromwell's plan. This army came to be called the " New Model Army."

In 1649 Charles I. was captured and executed. His son, Charles II., succeeded in raising another army in Scotland, but was defeated by Cromwell at the battle of Worcester in 1651.

Charles then fled to Flanders and Cromwell was left master of Britain, which he ruled until his death in 1658. The New Model Army, instead of being disbanded, was kept up as a regular army.

When Charles II. fled to Flanders, which was then in the hands of Spain, he was followed by a number of loyal officers and men. From amongst these men Charles, with the permission of the King of Spain, raised, for the protection of his person, a regiment which he called "The Royal Regiment of Guards." The men were mostly of gentle birth, and the Colonel was Lord Wentworth. This was the beginning of the regiment we know as the Grenadier Guards.

Grenadier Guards. After the Restoration of Charles II. in 1660 one of his first acts was to disband Cromwell's New Model Army. He decided, however, to raise a new Royal Army and he commenced by raising regiments of Guards for himself. To effect this a regiment of Guards of twelve companies was raised, and to them was added Lord Wentworth's regiment of Guards which, as has been seen, was raised abroad. As this regiment was composed of men who had been faithful to the King, it was given precedence as the senior regiment of Foot, and in 1685 it became known as the "First Regiment of Foot Guards."

Coldstream Guards. For the origin of the Coldstream Guards we must look to the opposite side of the Civil War. When, in 1650, Cromwell was sent to fight in Scotland, he took with him on his staff a Devon gentleman named George Monck, a prisoner from the Royalists.

Being anxious to give Monck a regiment, and no regiment being available, he made one for him by taking five companies from each of two regiments of the New Model Army. This became known as Monck's Regiment.

Colonel Monck was later promoted to General, and became the most able and powerful of Cromwell's generals.

At the time of Cromwell's death in 1658, Monck was

commanding the troops in Scotland and had with him there, amongst others, his own regiment. At this time confusion and misgovernment prevailed in London, and Monck decided to take matters into his own hands. He concentrated his forces at a village called Coldstream and then marched south to London.

When he reached London he dissolved Parliament and set up a new one. One of the first acts of this new Parliament was to invite Charles II. to return to England as King.

When the New Model Army was disbanded Monck's regiment was ordered to lay down its arms. This, though nominally carried out, did not actually happen, for the regiment was ordered to take up arms again as a regiment of the King. The regiment was constituted a regiment of Guards, being granted precedence next after the " Royal Regiment of Guards," or, as we know it, the Grenadier Guards.

During the lifetime of General Monck, who was created Duke of Albemarle, the regiment was known as the " Lord General's Regiment of Foot Guards." After Monck's death the regiment became known as the " Coldstream Guards," a name derived from the village from which Monck had commenced his march to London in 1660.

Scots Guards. In November, 1660, Charles II. commissioned the Earl of Linlithgow to raise for him in Scotland a regiment of Scottish Foot Guards, and in 1662 this regiment had reached a strength of seven companies. Until 1686 the Scots Guards were kept in Scotland, in which country they took part in various operations against the Covenantors.

In 1686 one Battalion was brought to London, and for the first time, was brigaded with the Grenadier and Coldstream Guards. During the wars of William III. the Scots Guards were brigaded with the other two regiments. They were not, however, finally incorporated in the Brigade of Guards until the Union of England and Scotland in 1707, when they were placed on the same footing as the Grenadier and Coldstream

Guards, and were given the name of the "Third Guards."

William IV., in 1834, conferred upon them the title of "Scots Fusilier Guards," and, in 1887, Queen Victoria restored to the regiment its original designation of the "Scots Guards."

Charles II. 1660. In 1665 war broke out with the Dutch, and several companies of the First Guards and the Coldstream were detached for service as marines with the fleet, and took part in various sea fights.

In 1677 a mixed Battalion of the First and Coldstream Guards was sent to Virginia, to suppress a revolution which had broken out in that colony. These were the first troops of the Standing Army to cross the Atlantic.

In 1689 a British force was sent to Tangier to defend it against the Moors. The Battle of "Tangier 1689" is the first of the battle honours on the colours of the First and Coldstream Guards.

James II. 1685. In 1685 the First and the Coldstream Guards took part in the Battle of Sedgemoor, when the Duke of Monmouth, who had rebelled against the King, was defeated.

William III. and Mary. 1689. When war broke out with France in 1689 the Brigade was sent to Flanders. This was the first occasion on which the Brigade fought on the Continent.

In 1695 King William besieged Namur, and the Brigade took a distinguished part in this celebrated siege.

Queen Anne 1702 Queen Anne's reign saw some of the greatest victories of the British Army. In 1702 war broke out again with France, and the British forces were dispatched to the Low Countries under the command of the Duke of Marlborough, one of the greatest British leaders of all time.

During this campaign the Brigade took part in the famous battles of Blenheim, Ramillies, Oudenarde and Malplaquet, all of which are among their battle honours.

A composite Battalion of the Brigade also formed part of an expedition which was sent to Portugal in 1704, and thence to Gibraltar.

The Coldstream took part in the successful defence of the fortress which is commemorated on their colours by the honour "Gibraltar." In 1713 the Peace of Utrecht put an end to the war, and the troops returned to England.

George I. 1714. The reign of George I. was, on the whole, a quiet one, though war broke out with Spain in 1718, and in the following year an expedition, which included the Brigade, was sent to that country. It landed at Vigo, but effected little beyond the capture of the town, and returned to England afterwards.

George II. 1727. In 1742 war broke out with France, and a British Army once more crossed the sea to the Low Countries. All three regiments of the Brigade took part in this campaign and fought in the battles of Dettingen, 1743, and Fontenoy, 1745. This war went on until 1748, when it was ended by the Treaty of Aix-la-Chapelle.

In 1756 war broke out again: this war with France was known as the "Seven Years War." The Brigade was sent to France again, but achieved nothing worthy of note. Soon after this, however, the Brigade was sent as part of an expedition to Germany.

George III. 1760. The Seven Years War ended in 1763: after this the Guards did not see active service for thirteen years.

In 1775, however, the American Colonies rebelled against Great Britain, and an army was sent across the Atlantic to quell the rebellion.

During the war the Brigade took part in the defeats of Brandywine, Guildford Court House and the surrender of Yorktown. The war concluded with the Treaty of

Versailles, 1783, England recognising the complete independence of the American Colonies. After this followed another eleven years of peace.

1793 saw England again at war with France, and the Brigade was sent to Flanders. In that same year the Brigade took part in the battle of Lincelles at which the French were defeated. This campaign ended in 1795, but war was soon to start again.

In 1799 the British Government decided to attack once more the French on the Continent, and a British force was sent to Holland to act in alliance with the Russians. Four battalions of Guards accompanied this expedition. The outstanding battle in this short campaign, in which the Brigade took part, was the battle of Egmont-op-Zee.

The next important event in the history of the Brigade was the expedition to Egypt in 1801. This campaign is commemorated on the Colours of the Coldstream and Scots Guards by the " Sphinx " superscribed " Egypt."

In March the Peace of Amiens was signed, which gave a breathing space in the long war with France.

It soon, however, became evident that Napoleon Bonaparte, First Consul of France, was only using the Peace in order to make preparations for further conquests, and in 1803 war was again declared against France.

Napoleon's object was an invasion of England ; his desire was, however, frustrated when the French Fleet was utterly destroyed by Nelson at Trafalgar on Oct. 21, 1805.

The danger of invasion now being over, the British Government began to consider how it could best attack the French abroad. Expeditions, in which the Brigade took part, were sent to Sicily, Germany and Denmark, but none of these expeditions effected anything of any importance.

The next great struggle which concerned the Brigade was the Peninsular War. The French had overrun Spain and Portugal, and the British Government willingly decided to send an army, under the Duke of Wellington, to the Peninsula, to help the Spaniards and Portuguese to drive out the invaders.

This great war with France lasted over a period of twenty years and ended in 1814.

The battles which occurred during this war, the names of which are emblazoned on the Colours of the Grenadier, Coldstream and Scots Guards, are : Corunna, Talavera, Barrosa and Fuentes d'Onor.

After the war Napoleon abdicated, and was exiled in the island of Elba in the Mediterranean.

On February 26th, 1815, however, Napoleon escaped from Elba, and, landing in France, was received there with enthusiasm.

At the end of March he once more entered Paris as Emperor, and at first attempted to make terms with his enemies. The Powers of Europe, however, refused to negotiate with him, and declared war against him as a public enemy.

The British and Prussians began to assemble their forces in Belgium, with a view to an invasion of France, and the Duke of Wellington took command of the British Army in the field.

The campaign which followed is known as "The Hundred Days," and it saw the final overthrow of Napoleon.

The great and final battle of this war was the battle of Waterloo, June 18th, 1815.

The Brigade greatly distinguished itself on this occasion, and the Duke of Wellington, in his despatch after the battle, stated : "The Army never upon any occasion conducted itself better. The Division of Guards set an example which was followed by all." After the Battle of Waterloo there followed a long period of European peace, which lasted until 1854.

George IV. 1820. During this reign an expedition, which included the Coldstream and Scots Guards, was sent to assist the Portuguese Government to suppress an insurrection and restore order in the country ; they returned home in 1827 having had no fighting.

William IV. 1830. This reign was peaceful and devoid of incident, but two events concerning the Brigade are worthy of record ; in 1833 the King granted the bearskin cap to the Coldstream and Scots Guards, thus making their dress the same as the Grenadiers, and in 1834 he conferred upon the Third or Scots Guards the title of " Scots Fusilier Guards," by which title the regiment continued to be known for forty years.

Queen Victoria. 1837. In 1854 the long peace came to an end when England and France declared war against Russia, and there followed what is known as the Crimean War.

During this war the Brigade played a very distinguished part and fought in the famous battles of Alma, Inkerman, and the Siege of Sevastopol. After the fall of Sevastopol active operations ceased, and in July, 1856, the Brigade returned home.

After the Crimean War came another long period of peace, broken only by the Indian Mutiny, in which the Brigade took no part. The next campaign that concerned the Brigade was the expedition to Egypt in 1882. Here the Guards Brigade, under the command of H.R.H. The Duke of Connaught,* defeated the Egyptians at Tel-el-Kebir, and then occupied Cairo.

In 1884 the British were sent to the Soudan to quell the rising of the Arabs. A composite regiment, consisting of one company from each Battalion of the Brigade of Guards, was formed for this service. The men were mounted on camels and the regiment was called " The Guards Camel Regiment." During this campaign the Brigade took part in the battle of Suakin, 1885.

Thirteen years later the Brigade was to see more service in Egypt. It took part in the Nile Expedition under Sir Herbert Kitchener,† being present at the Battle of Khartoum and the subsequent occupation of that city.

* Senior Colonel of the Brigade of Guards.

† Afterwards Field Marshal Earl Kitchener, Colonel of the Irish Guards from November 15th, 1914, to June 5th, 1916.

In the following year, 1899, war broke out with the Transvaal and the Orange Free State, and amongst the first troops to be sent to South Africa was a Guards Brigade.

During the Boer War the Brigade took part in the following battles :—Belmont, Modder River, Magersfontein, Bloemfontein, the capture of Pretoria and Diamond Hill.

In October, 1902, the Brigade returned to England.

On the 27th October, 1902, King Edward VII. inspected the Battalions of the Brigade who had taken part in the South African War. Amongst the troops on parade was the Irish Guards Section of Mounted Infantry which had taken part in the later stages of the war. They were led past His Majesty by the Colonel of the Regiment, Lord Roberts.

This, then, brings Brigade history up to the time of the formation of the Irish Guards.

From 1902 until the Great War of 1914 the Brigade carried out the normal duties of peace.

CHAPTER II.

The Origin of the Irish Regiments.

The Royal Irish Regiment (18th Foot).
The Royal Inniskilling Fusiliers (now forms part of the Royal Irish Fusiliers).
The Royal Irish Rifles (now the Royal Ulster Rifles, 83rd and 86th Foot).
The Royal Irish Fusiliers (87th Foot).
The Connaught Rangers (88th and 94th Foot).
The Prince of Wales' Leinster Regiment (100th and 109th Foot).
The Royal Munster Fusiliers (101st and 104th Foot).
The Royal Dublin Fusiliers (102nd and 103rd Foot).
5th (Royal Irish) Lancers.
6th (Inniskilling)Dragoons.
8th King's Royal Irish Hussars.

THE ROYAL IRISH REGIMENT.

(Disbanded 1922.)

The Royal Irish Regiment was raised on April 1st, 1684, by Charles II., when he reorganised the military forces in Ireland. The forces had hitherto consisted of a regiment of "Foot Guards"* and a number of "independent" troops of cavalry and companies of infantry, maintained to garrison various important points in the island.

THE ROYAL INNISKILLING FUSILIERS.

(Disbanded 1922.)

This regiment, long known as the 27th Inniskillings dates officially from New Year's Day, 1690, when the three regiments of foot of the Inniskilling Forces, afterwards joined into one, were taken into "pay and entertainment" by William III.

* For the history and origin of this Regiment see the Introduction.

The regiment was placed under the command of Colonel Tiffen, and it fought with great bravery throughout William's Irish campaign, from the passage of the Boyne to the fall of Limerick.

The 2nd Battalion Royal Inniskilling Fusiliers was the old 3rd Madras European Regiment.

This regiment later became the 108th Madras Infantry, and with the introduction of the Territorial System was again changed into the 2nd Battalion of the Royal Inniskilling Fusiliers.

THE ROYAL IRISH RIFLES.

The 1st Battalion Royal Irish Rifles was the original 83rd (County of Dublin) Regiment of Foot.

This regiment was raised in Dublin in 1793 by Colonel William Fitch, and numbered the 83rd Foot.

The 2nd Battalion was the old 86th (Royal County Down) Regiment.

This regiment was raised in Shropshire, Lancashire and the West Riding of Yorkshire by Colonel Cornelius Cuyler, under the title of The Shropshire Volunteers, and was ranked as the 86th Foot.

THE ROYAL IRISH FUSILIERS (PRINCESS VICTORIA'S.)

The 1st Battalion Royal Irish Fusiliers was the old 87th (Prince of Wales' Irish) Regiment of Foot.

This corps was raised in Ireland, under an order dated 18th September, 1793, by Colonel John Doyle, an officer who had served with much distinction in the old 105th (King's Irish) in the American War.

A second battalion of the 87th was raised in Ireland in 1804. This battalion subsequently won great fame during the Peninsular War under Colonel Gough.

The first French Eagle to be taken in this campaign was captured by the charge of the 87th at Barrosa. This was the Eagle of the famous 8th Regiment and the gift to the regiment of Napoleon himself.

After the battle General Graham wrote to Sir John

Doyle, the Colonel of the 87th Regiment :—" Your regiment has covered itself with glory. Recommend it, and its commander to their illustrious patron, the Prince Regent ; too much cannot be done for it."

The result of these recommendations was that the 87th was honoured by the Prince Regent with the title of the Prince of Wales' Own Irish Regiment, and it was allowed to bear as a Badge of Honour upon the Regimental Colours and appointments an Eagle with a wreath of laurel above the harp, in addition to the Arms of His Royal Highness.

The Commanding Officer, Major Gough (afterwards Field Marshal Viscount Gough), was recommended for promotion and received the brevet rank of Lieut.-Colonel. The captured Eagle was placed in the chapel of Chelsea Hospital, where it remained until April 16th, 1852, when it was stolen—whether by a patriotic Frenchman or by a thief, has never been discovered. All that remains of it is a gold leaf from the wreath, which was loose when the Eagle was captured, and which was detached by the Commanding Officer and sent to his wife. This leaf is now in the possession of Lieut.-Col. the Viscount Gough, M.C., Commanding the 1st Bn. Irish Guards, who is a great-grandson of the first Lord Gough.

The 2nd Battalion Royal Irish Fusiliers traces its origin from the 89th Foot. This regiment was raised in 1793 by Colonel Crosbie.

THE CONNAUGHT RANGERS.

(Disbanded 1922.)

The 1st Battalion was raised, under an order dated September 25th, 1793, by Colonel Thomas de Burgh, afterwards Earl of Clanricarde. It was chiefly recruited from Connaught, and was therefore styled The Connaught Rangers.

The 2nd Battalion traces its origin from the 94th Regiment of Foot. This regiment was raised in 1823 and, on the institution of the Territorial System in 1881, became the 2nd Battalion of The Connaught Rangers.

THE PRINCE OF WALES' LEINSTER REGIMENT (ROYAL CANADIANS).

(Disbanded 1922.)

The 1st Battalion of the Regiment owes its origin to Canadian loyalty at the time of the Indian Mutiny, 1857. An offer was made by a number of Canadian Volunteers to raise a regiment for service in India. This offer was accepted, and the regiment was formed and taken on the strength of the British Army as the 100th Prince of Wales' Royal Canadains.

The 2nd Battalion was the original Bombay Fusiliers, who were raised in Poona in 1853. They afterward became the 3rd Bombay European Infantry, and on the institution of the Territorial System in 1881 became the 2nd Battalion of the Leinster Regiment.

THE ROYAL MUNSTER FUSILIERS.

(Disbanded 1922.)

The 1st Battalion of the regiment dates its existence from 1756.

Certain independent companies and detachments, which had seen service in India in previous years, were formed into a battalion by Clive under the title of the Bengal European Regiment. In 1840 a second Bengal European Regiment was formed, and it afterwards became the 2nd Battalion of The Munster Fusiliers.

The 1st Battalion was in South Africa at the outbreak of the war, and the 2nd Battalion was in India.

THE ROYAL DUBLIN FUSILIERS.

(Disbanded 1922.)

From the reign of Charles I. to the middle of the reign of George II. the British factories along the south-east coast of India maintained companies of European Foot for the purpose of local defence.

In 1748 these independent companies, the oldest of which dated from 1645, were formed into a battalion five hundred strong. They were formed under the famous Stringer Lawrence, and called the Madras European Regiment. It is from this old regiment that the 1st Battalion The Royal Dublin Fusiliers trace their origin.

The 2nd Battalion of The Royal Dublin Fusiliers was originally the Bombay Regiment. This corps dates its origin from 1661, when the regiment was formed to garrison Bombay.

In 1849 the Bombay Regiment was formed into a Corps of Fusiliers in recognition of its distinguished services.

On the institution of the Territorial System the regiment became the 2nd Battalion The Royal Dublin Fusiliers.

5th (ROYAL IRISH) LANCERS.

(Disbanded 1922.)

The 5th (Royal Irish) Lancers represent the first of the two regiments of Dragoons, forming part of the Inniskilling Forces which did good service in the Irish War in the days of William of Orange.

It was the regiment of Colonel John Wynne, and became the Royal Irish Regiment of Dragoons, afterwards the 5th (Royal Irish) Dragoons.

The second regiment, commanded by Colonel Echlin, retained the name of Inniskilling Dragoons, and later became the 6th Inniskilling Dragoons.

The 5th (Royal Irish) Dragoons was disbanded in 1799, but was revived by Queen Victoria in 1858, under the rank and style of the 5th (Royal Irish) Lancers.

6th (INNISKILLING) DRAGOONS.

See under 5th (Royal Irish) Lancers.

8th KING'S ROYAL IRISH HUSSARS.

This regiment was formed in 1693 of Irish protestants and was commanded by Colonel Henry Cunningham ; hence it was known as Cunningham's Dragoons.

In 1777 the regiment was directed to be styled the 8th, or King's Own Royal Irish Regiment of Light Dragoons. It was known under this name for many years until 1822, when it was changed into a Hussar regiment and became the 8th King's Royal Irish Hussars.

CHAPTER III.

The Irish Regiments in the South African War.

Before commencing to describe the South African War and the part played in it by the Irish regiments, it will be as well to say something of the history of South Africa and the events that led up to the war.

The first European settlements round the Cape of Good Hope were made by the Dutch in 1657. These were conquered by Great Britain in 1795 and remained in our possession. Before long English settlers made their homes there, but they were outnumbered by the old Dutch farmers, or Boers, and did not get on well with them.

The whole history of South Africa has been fraught with disputes between the British and the Dutch, and the result has been to retard considerably its prosperity.

In 1836 the Boers, tiring of the English, moved into the interior, where they set up two independent Republics, the Transvaal and the Orange Free State, which were long suffered to remain independent.

In 1877, however, owing to troubles between the Boers and the Native States, the British Government intervened and annexed the country. The annexation of their country was greatly resented by the Boers. They had by this time greatly increased in numbers, and were determined not to submit to British rule, and so in 1880 war was declared.

A British force, under Sir George Colley, was sent to Natal, but was defeated at Laings Nek and subsequently at Majuba Hill. In 1881 peace was made and a treaty signed. By the treaty the Boers were given their independence, and the country was placed under the suzerainty of the British Crown.

In 1884 rich mines of diamonds and gold were discovered in the Transvaal. This now brought many English and other nationalities into the country, but the refusal of the Boers to grant these "Uitlanders" (foreigners) electoral rights and privileges excited the greatest discontent.

An abortive rebellion in 1895 (the Jameson Raid) gave the Transvaal Government a pretext for upholding this policy. Negotiations produced no results. Reinforcements were sent out to the British garrisons, and in October, 1899, the Governments of the Transvaal and the Orange Free State declared war on Great Britain.

It was reckoned that the Boers could put in to the field about 60,000 men, all of them mounted and most of them good marksmen. The whole of the British force in South Africa in October, 1899, did not exceed 22,000 men, and every preparation was at once made for the reinforcement of this small body.

In the following account of the war it will be seen that many regiments were employed almost entirely in column work or garrison duty.

The Boer was renowned for his mobility, he was artful and wily and knew the country well. Most of the fighting took place in very difficult country, and the unremitting strain of watching and of outpost duty was a severe tax on men's endurance and nerves.

Where casualities are mentioned it may seem to some that they are small and hardly worthy of mention. The enormous casualities of the Great War have tended to alter our perspective with regard to other wars.

It will be seen that some of the regiments had more work than others, and therefore had a better chance of distinguishing themselves, but we must remember that it is to the bravery of all the Irish regiments to which we owe our existence as Irish Guardsmen, and not to any particular one.

The South African War, 1899–1902. Immediately after the outbreak of the war the Transvaal Boers invaded Natal, and concentrated their forces in the neighbourhood of Laings Nek, the scene of our defeat in 1880.

The first British troops to be actually fired on by the Boers were a Mounted Infantry section of the Royal Dublin Fusiliers. The Dublin Fusiliers were stationed at Glencoe and formed part of a Brigade commanded by General Penn-Symons. In this Brigade were also the Royal Irish Fusiliers.

Talana Hill. Soon after the fighting commenced the Boers occupied Talana Hill. Both the Dublin Fusiliers and the Irish Fusiliers took part in the subsequent attack on Talana Hill, the Royal Irish suffering many casualties. During this action General Symons, the Brigade Commander, was killed.

Elaandslaagte. Meanwhile at Elaandslaagte General Sir George White successfully attacked the Boers, and enabled General Yule, who had succeeded General Symons, to fall back on Ladysmith. In this action the 5th (Royal Irish) Lancers greatly distinguished themselves, and took part in the one real cavalry charge of the war.

On October 22nd the retirement on Ladysmith began. and the Royal Irish Fusiliers felt the hardships of that march more than any other battalion, as they had no transport and had to carry all their baggage and ammunition.

During the retirement the 5th (Royal Irish) Lancers were in action again at Rietfontein, where they held the ridges and protected Sir George White's right flank. General White was now compelled to fall back, and within three days found himself beleaguered in his advanced base at Ladysmith.

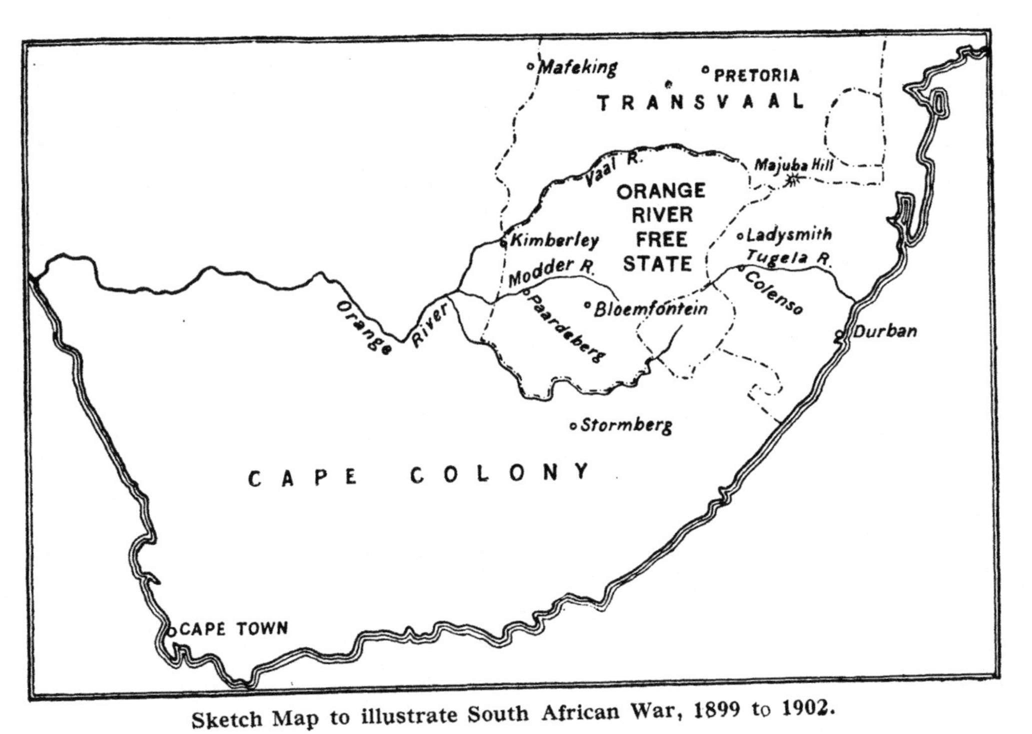

Sketch Map to illustrate South African War, 1899 to 1902.

Ladysmith Besieged. After the reverse at Lombards Kop, where the 5th Lancers again distinguished themselves. General French* commanding the mounted troops now thought that Ladysmith would be blockaded. Realising that mounted troops would be of very little use in a beleagured town, he managed to escape with his staff by the last train, actually under the enemy's fire.

Both battalions of the Dublin Fusiliers took part in the relief operations at Ladysmith, and two companies of the Royal Irish Fusiliers held " Red Hill " and " Range Post," two very important positions during the siege.

That same month General Sir Redvers Buller, V.C., arrived in South Africa and assumed command of the First Army Corps. In attempting to relieve the beleaguered garrison he sustained a severe reverse at Colenso, a town about 50 miles south of Ladysmith.

It was at Colenso that Lord Roberts' son—Captain F. Roberts, King's Royal Rifle Corps, lost his life in an attempt to save the guns of the 14th and 66th Batteries R.F.A. from capture. For his gallantry he received the posthumous award of the Victoria Cross. The Connaught Rangers were in the thick of the fight, and their losses were very heavy, amounting to 26 killed and 103 wounded. The Battalion fought magnificently, and was mentioned in General Buller's dispatch. The 2nd Battalion Dublin Fusiliers also distinguished themselves, and took part in the main assault on the Boer position. The Battalion also suffered very heavy casualties.

The first effort to relieve Ladysmith having failed, General Buller now made a further attempt. In his second attempt he managed to cross the Tugela, but retired without gaining his objective. During this attempt the Irish Fusiliers were engaged at Springfield Bridge on the Little Tugela.

* Afterwards F. M. the Earl of Ypres, Colonel of Irish Guards 1916–25.

Spion Kop. In a third attempt General Buller captured a commanding height called Spion Kop, but was subsequently forced to withdraw from it. The Connaught Rangers took part in this action, and suffered severely.

Pieters Hill. On February 23rd, 1899, a high, steep hill, strongly fortified, called Pieters Hill, was attacked by the Irish Brigade commanded by General Hart. The attacking regiments were the Royal Inniskilling Fusiliers, the Connaught Rangers and the Dublin Fusiliers. The attack was delivered with the utmost gallantry, but the men failed to reach the top. Mr. Winston Churchill, in his book, " My Early Life," describes this attack : " The spectacle was tragic. Through our glasses we could see the Boers' heads and slouch hats in miniature silhouette, wreathed and obscured by shell bursts against the evening sky. Up the bare grassy slopes slowly climbed the brown figures and glinting bayonets of the Irishmen. The climbing figures dwindled ; they ceased to move ; they vanished into the darkening hillside. Out of the twelve hundred men who assaulted, both Colonels, three Majors, twenty-six officers and six hundred soldiers had fallen killed or wounded."

The Relief of Ladysmith, February 28th, 1899. Two days later Ladysmith was relieved, and Lord Dundonald, with his cavalry Brigade, entered the town which had been besieged for one hundred and twenty days.

In recognition of their splendid services in the relief operations, the Dublin Fusiliers were specially selected to march into Ladysmith at the head of the relieving column.

The importance of the stubborn defence of Ladysmith cannot be overestimated. It completely disorganised the Boer plan of capturing Durban.

Meanwhile, in the Orange Free State, General Lord Methuen, a Scots Guardsmen and present Colonel of that regiment, advanced with a large column to the relief of Kimberley, which was also being besieged by the Boers.

Belmont, November 23rd, 1899. On November 23rd the Boer position at Belmont was successfully attacked. The 1st Battalion Royal Munster Fusiliers took part in the storming of Belmont.

The Guards Brigade was also present at this action.

Modder River, November 28th, 1899. Lord Methuen next attacked the Boer position at Modder River, and after a protracted engagement lasting twelve hours, drove the Boers back and crossed the river. In this action the Guards Brigade took an active part and " Modder River " is amongst the Battle Honours of the Grenadier, Coldstream and Scots Guards.

One squadron of the 6th (Inniskilling) Dragoons was present here and took part in the expedition to Koodooberg Drift and in the subsequent relief of Kimberley.

Magersfontein, December 11th, 1899. After crossing the Modder River, Lord Methuen attacked the Boer lines at Magersfontein, where the Guards Brigade was again engaged and suffered severely. Lord Methuen was unable to carry the position, and the British force was withdrawn to Modder River, having suffered a decided reverse. Lord Methuen's force was now forced to remain inactive for two months, watching the Boer position at Magersfontein.

Stormberg. In the northern part of Cape Colony, General Gatacre, while endeavouring to check the Boer invasion, made an unsuccessful attack on the Boers at Stormberg, with a heavy loss of prisoners and wounded. The Royal Irish Rifles formed part of General Gatacre's division, and took part in the battle of Stormberg.

The battalion fought gallantly against overwhelming numbers, suffering many casualties, over 200 men being taken prisoners. Shortly after this another unfortunate incident occurred to the battalion. The Boers came upon a detachment, which consisted of 3 Companies of the Royal Irish Rifles and 2 Companies of Mounted Infantry, and the whole force was compelled to surrender.

At this stage of the war, the enemy's ability in making sudden raids on isolated posts had not been fully appreciated.

Lord Roberts in Command About this time a large number of reinforcements were sent to the Cape from England, and the supreme command was entrusted to Lord Roberts, with Lord Kitchener as Chief of Staff.

Relief of Kimberley, February, 1900. On February 15th, 1900, Kimberley was relieved by General French with three cavalry brigades. It was here that French ordered two of his brigades to charge in successive lines in open order. This charge by galloping cavalry proved too much for the undisciplined Boers, who scattered on all sides and so allowed French to enter the town. One squadron of the 6th (Inniskilling) Dragoons took part in this charge.

After the relief of Kimberley the Boers fled eastwards to Bloemfontein. Shortly after, Lord Roberts cleverly turned the enemy's position at Magersfontein, and forced Cronje, the Boer leader, to retreat.

Paardeburg, February, 1900. At Paardeburg, Cronje, after some fierce fighting, surrendered unconditionally with 4,000 men. This was the anniversary of the Boer victory at Majuba Hill in 1880.

Bloemfontein, March 13th, 1900. Roberts now began his march to Bloemfontein, which he entered without opposition on March 13th, 1900. Neither the Guards Brigade nor the Irish regiments took part in the action at Paardeburg, but the Brigade was present at the actions of Poplar Grove and Drietfontein, and took part in the advance to Bloemfontein, making a fine march of 40 miles in 26 hours.

After the occupation of Bloemfontein the Orange Free State was formally annexed to the British Empire under the name of the "Orange River Colony."

Relief of Mafeking, May 17th, 1900.

Meanwhile, in the Western Transvaal, Mafeking, which had been besieged for two hundred and fifteen days, was relieved by Colonel Bryan Mahon* with a mounted column. Colonel Mahon had only recently given up the command of the 8th (Royal Irish) Hussars.

It was at Mafeking that Captain C. FitzClarence, of the Royal Fusiliers, gained the Victoria Cross for great gallantry when in command of a squadron of Protectorate troops. Captain FitzClarence joined the Irish Guards on their formation, and rose to be Lieutenant-Colonel Commanding the Regiment. He was killed near Ypres in 1914 while in command of the 1st Guards Brigade.

During the advance of the Mafeking relief force the Connaught Rangers and a part of the Dublin Fusiliers acted as covering force to the column.

Capture of Pretoria, June 5th, 1900.

Now that Ladysmith, Kimberley and Mafeking had been relieved, Lord Roberts, with the main body of his force (including the Guards Brigade), marched northwards from Bloemfontein. After a certain amount of fighting he entered Pretoria, the capital of the Transvaal, on June 5th, 1900.

To return again to Natal, after General Buller had relieved Ladysmith, he continued his advance to Bergendal, Machadodorp, and Lyndenberg. The Inniskilling Fusiliers took part in this march and gained great praise in the action at Bergendal on August 27th, 1900. General Buller's dispatch of November 9th, 1900, after referring to the battalion's very severe losses, remarks, "There can, I think, be but few instances in

* Afterwards General the Rt. Hon. Sir Bryan Mahon, K.C.B., K.C.V.O., a Senator of the Irish Free State and a Privy Councillor for Ireland.

history in which a Battalion, after such heavy losses, has returned a perfect machine into the fighting line in so short a time."

In the march from Machadodorp to Heidleberg the 8th (King's Royal Irish) Hussars became heavily engaged near Geluk with a body of 1,100 Boers and four guns. Although very hardly pressed they succeeded in holding their own until General French came to their assistance.

Transvaal Annexed. After the capture of Pretoria, President Kruger of the Transvaal Republic fled to Europe, and three months later Lord Roberts issued a proclamation annexing the Transvaal.

It was generally considered that, with the fall of Pretoria, the war would end. This, however, was far from being the case, for the Boers declined to sue for peace. The real trouble was only just beginning. The task of defending a line of communications 1,000 miles long against a highly mobile, skilful and cunning enemy was no light one. The enemy wore no uniforms, they mingled with the population ; it was impossible to know who was an enemy or who was friend, and then suddenly they would appear from nowhere and ride down on some column or isolated post.

Blockhouse Lines. In order to deal with this situation the British divided the country up with lines of blockhouses. The whole countryside was cleared of inhabitants, who were gathered into concentration camps. This was one of the most distressing periods of the war. Many Boer farms had to be burned by the British as acts of reprisal. Much ill feeling and bitterness was caused, which took a very long time to heal.

Lord Kitchener was in command during this period, and it needed all his skill and determination to carry the operations to a successful issue.

The British forces in South Africa now amounted to some 200,000 men. Amongst the regiments that had arrived in the latter part of 1900 were the Leinster

Regiment, the 2nd Battalion Munster Fusiliers, the Royal Irish Regiment, and the 2nd Battalion Inniskilling Fusiliers. The Leinster Regiment saw a great deal of fighting with the 16th Brigade, in which Brigade were also the 2nd Battalion Grenadier Guards and 2nd Battalion Scots Guards. The Leinsters were renowned for their good comradeship and cheerfulness.

In the Household Brigade Magazine for December, 1901, an officer of the Brigade of Guards, writing from the Brandwater Basin, said: " The Leinsters' garrison the blockhouses; they are splendid fellows, just as Irish as they can be, and they work like slaves, it doesn't matter whether it's a fort or on earthwork or a cask of rum, they'll go at it till it's finished."

During the first five months of 1902, while the series of great drives were taking place in Rundles district, the 1st battalion of the Leinsters did splendid work in holding lines and assisting columns. The 2nd Battalion of the Regiment was in the West Indies at the outbreak of the war. They arrived in South Africa in January, 1902, and took part in the latter period of the war.

When Belfast (Natal) was attacked on January 7th, 1901, the Royal Irish Regiment provided part of the garrison. After severe fighting the Boer attack was driven off.

General Ben Viljoen, the Boer commander during the attack on Belfast, mentions in his book on the campaign that the Royal Irish Regiment were the defenders, and says :—" of which regiment all Britain should be proud." It was at this attack that Private Barry of the Regiment won the Victoria Cross. Afterwards the Regiment operated in the Eastern Transvaal and did garrison duty at Lyndenburg until the end of the war.

In 1901 and 1902 a portion of the 5th (Royal Irish) Lancers were in Cape Colony and had a very hard time on the Zeekoe River, Lieutenant Dugdale being awarded the Victoria Cross for gallantry.

The 8th (King's Royal Irish) Hussars, during the latter stages of the war, saw a good deal of fighting from the Eastern Transvaal to the borders of Zululand.

The 2nd Battalion Dublin Fusiliers, which had been fighting constantly and had suffered so many casualties, was sent to Cape Colony during this phase of the operations and it remained there until the close of the war. The Battalion sailed from Durban in January, 1902, receiving a tremendous "send off" from the Natal folk, for whom they had fought so ungrudgingly. Out of the officers commencing the war at the battle of Talana Hill only one escaped unwounded.

During the closing stages of the war the Irish Regiments were employed on garrison and column duties. These duties were trying and arduous, and required much patience and endurance.

As regards the earlier stages of the war many omissions have no doubt been made, but the account is sufficient to show the splendid part the Irish Regiments played during the war.

Peace Signed, May, 1902. In May, 1902, after the war had lasted two years and seven months, peace was signed at Pretoria, and the Transvaal and the Orange Free State were annexed. A few years later free institutions were restored to them and they were joined to Cape Colony and Natal in the South African Union.

Two of the best Boer Generals, Botha* and Smuts†, accepted commands of British Armies in the Great War, and rendered most valuable service.

The loss of men on the side of the British in the war was estimated at 23,000, and the cost of the war upwards of 22 millions.

These figures make an interesting comparison with the Great War when it is realised that our losses at the first Battle of Ypres, between October 14th and November 30th, amounted to more than 58,000.

* General the Rt. Hon. Louis Botha, P.C. (deceased).

† Lieut.-General the Rt. Hon. Jan Christiaan Smuts, P.C., C.H., K.C., LL.D.

CHAPTER IV.

The Irish Guards Mounted Infantry Section.

A Mounted Infantry Company from the Brigade of Guards was formed in August, 1901, for service in South Africa. Each Regiment supplied one Section. A Section consisted of 1 officer (a subaltern), 1 serjeant, 1 drummer and 30 men.

The 1st Company Guards Mounted Infantry, as they were called, assembled at North Camp, Aldershot, for special instruction in Mounted Infantry work under the supervision of Lieutenant-Colonel Godley (Irish Guards).*

The Irish Guards Section was commanded by Lieutenant Lord Herbert Scott. The men, who had all been specially selected, were mostly "marksmen." Few of them had any idea of horse management or riding, but the necessary skill was very soon acquired.

An amusing story is told of one of the Section who, when asked whether the work was at all what he expected, replied, "Indeed not! Sure I thought there would be a horseman to look after my horse."

The Guards Mounted Infantry held the Mounted Infantry record for having been trained and passed fit for active service in the short space of six weeks.

On the 27th November, the Company was due to leave Aldershot for Southampton, and for embarkation on the troopship "Canada." The Company was inspected by Lord Roberts before it left Aldershot and it was given a great "send off."

On December 17th, 1901, the Company reached Cape Town. The Irish Guards Section received orders to join Colonel Crabbe's column in General French's force. The other three Sections were sent to Pretoria.

* Afterwards General Sir Alexander Godley, K.C.B., K.C.M.G.

On December 19th the Section entrained for Moorreesburg where it joined Colonel Crabbe.

The plan at this time was to push the Boers out of the Colony and drive them up against our line of blockhouses. It was no easy matter as the Boers could travel faster than our troops and used to double back round the flanks. It was the duty of the Mounted Infantry to try and prevent this.

The Boers had no transport. Our troops had to carry transport and guns. The country was most difficult, which made movement very slow, so it is easy to imagine what tiring and difficult work fell to the lot of the Mounted Infantry.

On November 11th a commando of about 200 Boers broke back through our columns, thereby gaining fresh stores and recruits. They took one day to cover a distance which took the Mounted Infantry four days.

The next eighteen months were spent by the Guards Mounted Infantry in trekking about the country, assisting and convoying columns and frequently being harassed by small parties of Boers.

On February 6th, 1902, Colonel Crabbe's column became heavily engaged at Uitspanfontien. The column was ambushed and although the casualties were heavy the Guards Mounted Infantry saved the situation by covering the retirement of the column.

The Boers were very daring and galloped our troops down with revolvers. Serjeant Hudson (Irish Guards Section), whilst trying to cover the retirement of his section, suddenly found himself cut off and surrounded by several Boers. He fixed his bayonet, as coolly as if he were on the parade ground, and charged a Boer who was doing a great deal of damage with a Mauser pistol. Unfortunately Serjeant Hudson's horse fell, and he was made prisoner, but managed later to escape.

This was the first engagement in which an Irish Guards section suffered casualties ; Guardsmen Byrne, Cairns, Durkin, Prendegast and McDermott were killed on that day.

There is little more to say about the Irish Guards Section. It remained in South Africa until peace was declared, returning to England on the 6th of October, 1902.

No. 2 Company, Guards Mounted Infantry, was also in South Africa during the later stages, the Irish Guards Section being commanded by Lieutenant H. F. Ward. This section did not have the same hard time that No. 1 Company had, but they acquitted themselves well on all occasions.

The four Irish Guardsmen who fell in the engagement on February 5th were buried on the veldt close to where they fell at Uitspanfontein. A stone was erected on the spot and a memorial tablet was also placed in St. Edward's Church, Palace Street, S.W.

On the 27th of October, 1902, King Edward inspected those Battalions of the Brigade who had been on active service in South Africa. Lord Roberts, as Colonel of the Irish Guards, led the Irish Guards Mounted Infantry Sections past His Majesty. No. 1 Section was commanded by Lord Herbert Scott and No. 2 Section by Lieutenant Ward.

Colour-Serjeant Hudson received the Distinguished Conduct Medal as a reward for the gallantry he had displayed at Uitspanfontein.

This, then, is the very brief account of the Irish Guards Section Mounted Infantry, who had the good fortune and honour of being the first Irish Guardsmen to serve their King and Country. The Officers, Non-commissioned Officers and Guardsmen of the newly-formed Irish Guards who took part in the operations in South Africa, showed that Irishmen could and would uphold the high tradition and standing of the " Brigade of Guards."

CHAPTER V.

How the Regiment was formed.

The Army Order announcing the formation of the Regiment was followed immediately by a War Office letter, in which it was stated that the new Regiment would be incorporated in the Brigade of Guards. It also authorized an establishment for two Companies.

The establishment for a battalion at that time was eight Companies, and it was not until a year later that the Irish Guards were augmented to that number.

The First Recruit. Immediately after the Army Order was published the whole of the Irish and Scottish Districts were thrown open for the raising of recruits for the Regiment, and on April 21st, 1900, the first recruit, James O'Brien, of Limerick, was enlisted.

The question now arose of procuring trained soldiers for the Regiment. A bounty of two pounds was given to all men of Irish nationality who were willing to transfer from the other regiments of the Brigade, and the following so transferred :—

From the Grenadiers : 2 Drummers and 71 men.
From the Coldstream : 2 Drummers and 52 men.
From the Scots Guards : 1 Drummer and 24 men.

Men from other Irish regiments also transferred in addition to those from the Brigade of Guards, and Regimental Number ONE was assigned to Colour-Serjeant Conroy, a transfer from the Munster Fusiliers.

The First Officers. The Officers of the Regiment were chosen from the other regiments of the Brigade. Lieut.-Colonel V. J. Dawson, Coldstream Guards, was appointed Lieutenant-Colonel Commanding the Regiment, and Lieut.-Colonel R. J. Cooper, Grenadier Guards, was appointed Officer Commanding the 1st Battalion. Lieut.-Colonel Cooper was the first officer to be gazetted to the Regiment.

In September, 1900, all English Districts were opened for Irishmen wishing to enlist, and the establishment of the Battalion was increased to four Companies.

On September 22nd, 1900, the formation of the 1st Battalion was commenced by the assembly at Pirbright of the Headquarters of the Battalion; the transfers from other regiments, and the recruits. On the same date a Regimental Orderly Room was opened at the Horse Guards, Whitehall, London.

Her Majesty The Queen now gave her approval to the Badge and uniform of the Regiment.

The Cap Badge. The Cap Badge is the Star of the Order of St. Patrick, and the motto "Quis Separabit" (Who will divide us?) and the date "1783," the date of the foundation of the Order of St. Patrick.

The First Colonel of the Regiment. In October, 1900, a great honour was conferred on the Regiment by the appointment of Field Marshal Lord Roberts, V.C., to be Colonel of the Regiment.

The First Guard of Honour. Lord Roberts was at that time still in South Africa and on his arrival in London in January, 1901, the Regiment furnished its first Guard of Honour at Paddington Station under the command of Major G. C. Nugent.* This was the first time that the Regiment had been "on view," and they certainly showed that they could be as smart and as well turned out as any other regiment of the Brigade.

Shortly after this the establishment of the Battalion was increased to six Companies.

When the Battalion arrived in London to do duty in the West End for the first time, it was quartered at Chelsea Barracks. It received a most enthusiastic welcome on its arrival. Everyone was anxious to see how the newly-formed regiment of the Brigade would

* Major Nugent was killed in action on 31st May, 1915. His son, Major T. E. G. Nugent, M.V.O., M.C., is serving with the Regiment.

look. The Londoner is extremely critical, but he was not disappointed.

The First King's Guard. The Regiment was now formed. It had done its first Guard of Honour, and on February 2nd, 1901, it took part in " Lining the Streets " for the funeral of Queen Victoria. On Sunday, March 3rd, 1901, the Battalion mounted King's Guard for the first time.

The Regiment had been " passed off the square," and from now on shared the many duties that are required of a battalion stationed in London. That same year the Mounted Infantry Section of the Regiment, about which we have read, was sent to South Africa.

Presentation of Colours. The next big event in the history of the Regiment was the Presentation of Colours by His Majesty King Edward VII. on May 30th, 1902.

May 30th was a fine and sunny day, and great crowds thronged to the Horse Guards Parade to see His Majesty present the first Colours to his new regiment of Foot Guards. H.M. The King, as Colonel-in-Chief, wore the uniform of the Regiment. The troops on parade were under the command of the Regimental Lieutenant-Colonel, Colonel V. J. Dawson.

It was the first occasion on which His Majesty had addressed the Regiment, and an extract of his speech is quoted below:

> " As your Sovereign, and as your Colonel-in-Chief, I confide to you, for the honour and glory of the Country and of the Regiment, these Colours.
>
> " May you, in this newly-formed Regiment, emulate the proud example of your brothers of the Grenadier, Coldstream and Scots Guards. I have little doubt all ranks are imbued with the same feelings as exist in the other three regiments, and I feel sure that although you are the youngest and last regiment of Guards, you will in no wise be the last."

These Colours were laid-up in the Guards' Chapel on March 20th, 1914, where they may now be seen.

St. Patrick's Day. In 1902 Her Majesty Queen Alexandra graciously consented to make the gift of Shamrock to the Regiment on St. Patrick's Day. The first parade took place that year at the Tower of London, and the Shamrock was presented by Lord Roberts, the Colonel of the Regiment. The ceremonial gift of Shamrock on St. Patrick's Day has now become an annual event.

When Her Majesty died in 1927, her grand-daughter, H.R.H. Princess Mary, continued the gift.

Coronation of King George V. The Battalion took part in "Lining the Streets" at the funeral of King Edward VII, and also at the Coronation of King George V on June 22nd, 1911.

In 1913 H.M. King George V presented new Colours to the Battalion. The ceremony took place in the gardens at Buckingham Palace. In his address to the Battalion His Majesty stated that the Regiment had yet had no opportunity of showing its fighting qualities, but that when it did, he knew that it would uphold the great traditions of the Brigade of Guards.

That opportunity came all too soon. In August 1914, just over a year later, the Battalion was in France with the Expeditionary Force.

SPORT IN THE BATTALION.

Boxing. It was not long after its formation that the Regiment made a name for itself in sport and athletics. The Regiment soon produced some very good boxers.

It would be impossible to mention Boxing without saying something about Colonel J. Fowles, first Quartermaster to the Irish Guards.

Colonel Fowles was one of the pioneers of Army boxing. When he enlisted in the Grenadiers in 1879, boxing was considered bad form. Those who attended fights not only ran the risk of taking an involuntary part, but also of appearing in the nearest Police Court for assisting in committing a breach of the peace.

Serjeant Fowles, as he then was, however, attended many of the old-time London prize-fights, and it appears he was very anxious even at this early date to arrange contests in Barracks. The Omdurman Campaign in Egypt, however, interfered with his plans, but on his return, with the help of others, he staged what was perhaps the first Army Championships at Burtons Court.

The show was a great success, and gave Fowles (now Drill Sergeant) a chance of showing his abilities as an organizer of boxing tournaments. Fowles not only arranged for professional instruction, but enlisted the aid of his amateur friends.

Shortly after this efforts were made to inaugurate Army Boxing Championships. In 1896 a start was made, which proved immediately the value of Fowles' enthusiasm, for the Grenadier Guards won every weight.

On the formation of the Irish Guards Fowles was gazetted Quarter-Master. His enthusiasm for boxing did not lessen with his new appointment. With new material he set to work, and, except for that initial period required to train his men, he soon promoted a high standard of boxing in the Regiment.

During his service in the Regiment he organized many tournaments at Windsor, Aldershot and the Tower of London. He had a great way of inducing men to fight, and he never failed to get competitors. When he arrived in the " Gym " on practice nights he would " pair off " his men to box as though he were detailing them on parade.

Fowles showed great delight when any of the team won a fight, but he did not hesitate to pour scorn on them when they were beaten, especially by the Scots Guards : " What the divil do ye mean by letting that Hielandman beat ye," he would say ; " Confound you, you boxed like an old woman to-night."

Amongst the many splendid boxers who developed their skill during this period were McLaughlin, Delaney, Farnam, Sinclair, Voyles, McEnroy and Killeen. All these men were great fighters. In those days Army boxers were allowed to fight professionals, and many fine fights took place between Irish Guardsmen and professionals.

The first representative of the Regiment to show promise was McLaughlin. A heavy-weight of undoubted fighting ability, he won a number of contests and competitions for the Battalion, and was recognised as one of the best men in the Services during his time—1903–1906.

Delaney, a light-weight, was another of the earlier products of the Regiment who could not only fight, but had a high standard of boxing ability.

Another boxer was Killeen, a middle-weight, who developed into one of the best men in the Services. Killeen afterwards went to America, where he became a professional. Had he remained in England, there is no doubt he would have become a champion.

Following hard on Killeen's heels at the same period was another middle-weight, Private Farnam. Modelled on the Killeen style of boxing and fighting, he was a difficult man to beat. He was known to waste 7 lbs. on the road in the morning and the same evening to beat one of the best men in the Services (Private Harris, 2nd Bn. Coldstream Guards) in four rounds. Farnam beat, amongst others, the famous Frank Craig (The Coffee Cooler) over 20 rounds in Dublin in 1909.

Private Voyles, afterwards C.S.M. Voyles, D.C.M., a later (1908) contemporary of Farnam's, developed into a first-class boxer. Voyles' best fight was against Bombardier Wells in an eliminating trial to find the champion of England. It was one of the best heavy-weight contests seen in England for years.

Voyles boxed in great style, and had Wells down for a long count. He left his corner in the 10th round with the set purpose of finishing his opponent. Wells, however, with the longer reach, got the better of him and won the fight. Wells went on to become champion of England.

Although Voyles won the Army and Navy Championships in 1911 and 1912 and several other important contests afterwards, he never again boxed with the same fire as he did against Wells.

Voyles was the first man to win an official Army and Navy Championship for the Regiment.

Private Sinclair, a welter-weight, was a most determined and skilful boxer. He won the Brigade Championship three years in succession. His best fight was at Windsor in 1909, when he beat Corporal Coles (West Yorkshire Regiment), then Army and Navy Champion, over 10 rounds.

The finest middle-weight the Regiment produced was Sergeant, now Captain, McEnroy. Starting boxing in 1909, he was finalist in the Army and Navy Championship every year from 1909—1914. He only succeeded in winning the official title one year, 1912.

That year he was selected to box an eliminating trial for the Championship of England against Sid Ellis. McEnroy knocked Ellis out in two rounds, and McEnroy was then matched against Jack Harrison (an ex-Grenadier) over 20 rounds for the Middle-weight Championship of England and the Lonsdale Belt. Harrison won on points after a close fight.

Although only a middle-weight, McEnroy has beaten amongst others Dennis Haugh and Harry Reeve, both of whom were Light-Heavy-Weight Champions and Lonsdale Belt Holders.

Besides being a fine boxer, McEnroy was at one time the best shot in the Aldershot Command.

The brothers Hickey were both fine fighters. One was rather a better boxer than the other. Joe Hickey entered for the Feather-Weight Army Championship in 1913, and met the renowned Dusty Miller. It was only after three strenuous rounds that Miller won the fight.

Amongst others who helped to add to the Regimental laurels in boxing were Corporal Donnelly, Corporal Campbell—who won the Brigade Welter-Weight—and Private Clifford.

Clifford went to Australia, where he became a prominent boxer. He returned to the Regiment on the outbreak of war and won many contests.

The best boxer which the Regiment has produced since the war is Guardsman McCall, who left the Regiment to become a professional and, as Steve McCall, won the Middle-Weight Championship of Scotland in 1930.

The Regiment won the H.B. Boxing Championship every year from 1925—1929.

Tug-of-War. Soon after the formation of the Regiment Colour Sergeant Foley, a keen tug-of-war enthusiast, got to work to train an Irish Guards team.

In 1902 the team entered for the Brigade Sports at Burtons Court, but it was not successful. The following year, however, it was successful and won the Brigade Cup.

The next year, when the Battalion was at Aldershot, the team, now coached by Drill Sergeant Hudson, who had been with the Mounted Infantry Section in South Africa, won the Brigade Cup again, and was also successful in the Aldershot Command Sports. This success qualified the team to enter for the Military Tournament, where it was beaten by the Royal Artillery team from Woolwich.

1906 saw the Battalion once more at Aldershot, where the team was again successful in the Command Sports. Shortly afterwards it beat a strong Police team which had never yet been beaten. From 1906 to 1914 the team continued its successes.

In 1917 the 2nd Battalion team won the final in the 31st Divisional Sports. After the war in Cologne, in Constantinople, in Gibraltar, as well as at home, the Irish Guards Tug-of-War Team was always able to give a good account of itself. Among the members of our great tug-of-war team were : Sergeant T. Murphy, Sergeant-Major Cahill, D.C.M., Drill Sergeant Hudson, Company Sergeant-Majors Proctor, Shea, Casey and Fitzgerald, all men of magnificent physique.

It is hoped that one day the past glories of the Irish Guards Tug-of-War Team may again be revived.

Athletics. It was not until about 1912 that the Regiment really began to make a name for itself on the running track.

Previous to this athletics in the Army had not been given great encouragement. Men ran more as professionals and were allowed to enter for any events they wished, for which they received prize money.

In 1919 the Army Athletic Association and Cross Country Association was formed.

The Regiment had, however, some very fine athletes even in the early days. C.Q.M. Sgt. P. Lowe won many events in the Brigade at distances from 440 yards to 1 mile from 1906—1911. He held the Guards Depot All-Round Championship during 1908–1909. J. J. Carroll and J. Nolan were also splendid runners. Nolan commenced his career by winning the Army Boys 200 yards Championship in 1910.

In 1912 the Regiment won the Lawson Cup, given to the winners of the Household Brigade Unit Team Championship, and continued to do so from that year until 1926.*

The success of the Battalion in this line was very largely due to two officers—Lieutenant E. B. Greer and Lieutenant the Hon. H. R. L. G. Alexander. These two officers joined the Regiment in 1911. Both fine athletes themselves, they set to work to encourage athletics in the Battalion.

In 1913 Lieutenant Greer won the Army ¼ Mile Championship and Lieutenant Alexander won the Mile Championship of Ireland in 1914.

In 1915 Lieut.-Colonel Greer and Colonel Alexander (as they afterwards became) formed the Irish Guards Athletic Club.

These two officers, together with Sergeant-Major Price and O.R. Colour-Sergeant Smythe, composed the first Committee. They immediately decided to secure the services of Harry Andrews as trainer. Harry Andrews was already well-known as a trainer, and he very soon proved his worth.

* The Battalion did not compete for the Lawson Cup in 1922–1923, as it was on Foreign Service during those years.

On August 4th, 1915, the team entered for and won the Marathon Race (open to the Army and Navy) at Stamford Bridge. After this the team won almost every event for which it entered, and so fine a team were they that they came to be known as the "Invincibles."

Amongst the fine runners which the Battalion produced were Corporal Elliott, one of the best mile runners, Corporals Gamble, Moran, Timmins, Sergeant Nolan, besides many others.

Corporal Elliott later obtained a commission in the Lancashire Fusiliers, and won the Distinguished Service Order and M.C. and bar while serving with them.

It was indeed a great loss to the Battalion when Lieut.-Colonel Greer was killed in 1917. Not only did we lose an extremely capable and popular officer, but one of the finest athletes in the Army.

Colonel Greer's short career had been one of brilliant promise. He had joined the Regiment three years before the war. This period of peace was marked by some notable achievements, in addition to many successes of a minor order.

In 1913 he won the ¼ Mile Championship of the Army at Aldershot, and the ¼ Mile in the Southern London Area Championships.

At the same time, while he thus achieved the highest distinctions on the running track, he promised to become a polo player and cross-country rider of first-class merit.

He was killed near Passchendaele on July 31st, 1917, while commanding the 2nd Bn. of the Regiment.

After the war the Irish Guards Athletic Team still continued its successes, and won many events. In 1919 Drill-Sergeant Murphy won the Army Long Jump Championship and Captain C. L. J. Bowen was awarded his Army Badge and Colours in 1925 for this event. Captain Bowen won the United Services Long Jump Championship in 1925.

The Battalion was the first to win the Army Unit Team Championship, which was first instituted in 1920.

In 1920 Sergeant Nolan won the Army 440 yards Championship, and in 1923 the Commanding Officer—Lieut.-Colonel Alexander—won the Brigade Mile in Constantinople.

Polo. The Irish Guards Polo Team won the Polo Challenge Cup, presented to the Brigade of Guards by Colonel V. J. Dawson, from 1902–1907. Amongst those who played polo for the Regiment during these years were Sir Hill Child, The Earl of Kerry, Lieut.-Colonel the Hon. G. H. Morris, Lieut. H. Ward, General Godley, Brig.-Gen. R. C. McCalmont.

A list of the Athletic and Boxing events which the Battalion has won since the war and up to 1929 is given in the Appendix.

CHAPTER VI.

Narrative History of the Irish Guards in the Great War - 1914 - 1918.

Causes of the War. The causes which led up to Great Britain going to war against Germany are far too long and complicated to be set out in this book. It is enough to say that war was declared on August 4th, 1914, consequent on the Germans violating the neutrality of Belgium and making war against France.

However, behind the natural desire of the English nation to fulfil its treaty obligations to the Belgians, there existed a fear that had lasted throughout the centuries. It was the fear of seeing a strong naval and military power established in the Low Countries, as Holland and Belgium are sometimes called.

Nearly all England's wars of the past have been fought for this same cause. Germany had for the last 25 years been England's chief commercial rival; her Army had always been thought to be supreme and her Navy was growing in size and efficiency every year.

It was impossible for the leaders of the British Nation to stand aloof and watch the almost certain destruction of France and Belgium. The whole future of the British was dependant on the ability of these two powers to maintain their independance.

Mobilization. As soon as war became inevitable general mobilization was ordered. During July, 1914, the 1st Bn. Irish Guards was quartered at Wellington Barracks, and on mobilization formed part of the 4th Guards Brigade.

The Brigade consisted of the following battalions :—

2nd Bn. Grenadier Guards.
2nd Bn. Coldstream Guards.
3rd Bn. Coldstream Guards.
1st Bn. Irish Guards.

and was commanded by Brig.-Genl. R. Scott-Kerr, Grenadier Guards. All officers had been recalled from leave and all furlough had been stopped on July 30th.

At 4 p.m. on August 4th a War Office telegram saying " Get on with it " was received in the Regimental Orderly Room. All the mobilization notices were posted immediately to every Irish Guards Reservist. The total number sent out was 1,322. A considerable number of Irish Guards Reservists were serving with the Royal Irish Constabulary at this time. These men all joined on mobilization. In addition to these, in November, 1914, two hundred men of the R.I.C., selected from a large number of volunteers, were specially chosen for enlistment into the Irish Guards. Most of these men joined the 2nd Battalion and afterwards did splendid work in the war. The Irish Guards had a very close connection with the R.I.C., and it was a sad day for the Regiment when it was disbanded in 1922.

The reservists began to come in early in the morning of August 5th. The first man to report was a Private Sales. He was killed in action in May, 1915. The majority of the men reported on August 6th. The greater number coming from their homes in Ireland.

Mobilization was practically completed by August 7th. The surplus Reservists were quartered at the Duke of York's School. These were afterwards moved to Warley Barracks near Brentwood, and became the 2nd (Reserve) Bn. Irish Guards, under the command of Lt.-Col. the Earl of Kerry, now the Marquis of Lansdowne.

Reservists also joined the Colours from all parts of the world. A large contingent arrived at Warley from Canada at the end of October, 1914, and from Australia in December, 1914.

On Sunday, August 9th, the whole Battalion attended Church Parade. The Roman Catholics paraded under the Commanding Officer, and went to Mass at Westminster Cathedral, where the sermon was preached by Cardinal Bourne.

At 8 a.m. on August 11th the Battalion marched to

Hyde Park, where it was inspected by the Colonel of the Regiment, Field Marshal Lord Roberts.

Next day the Battalion, under Lt.-Col. the Hon. G. H. Morris, entrained for Southampton at Nine Elms Station. That night the Battalion embarked on "s.s. Novara." On arrival next morning at Havre the troops were disembarked and marched to No. 2 Rest Camp, which was about 3 miles away.

Arrival at Havre.

They received a most enthusiastic welcome from the French as they passed through the town. The weather was very hot; the march coming as it did after a sleepless night at sea, was a very trying one.

Next day the Battalion entrained, with the remainder of the Brigade, for the British concentration area between Le Cateau and Guise.

The British Expeditionary Force was under the command of Field Marshal Sir John French, and was composed of four Divisions and a Cavalry Division. The 4th Guards Brigade formed part of the 2nd Division of the First Army Corps. The First Army Corps was commanded by General Sir Douglas Haig, and the 2nd Division by Major-General Sir Charles Monro.

THE RETREAT FROM MONS.

On August 21st, by order of General Joffre, the French Commander-in-Chief, the British Expeditionary Force moved forward on the left of the French Fifth Army towards the line of the River Sambre and the Mons-Conde Canal.

On the 22nd the French Fifth Army was heavily engaged on the Sambre and its centre was compelled to retire. As a result of this reverse on their right the advance of the British Forces had to be checked, and they were subsequently ordered to remain in position to assist the retirement of the French.

It was in the neighbourhood of Mons that the first clash of British and German arms took place early in the morning of August 23rd. It soon became apparent that General Joffre's offensive had failed.

The primary cause of the failure was due to the fact that the French in making their plans had never considered the possibility of the Germans violating the neutrality of Belgium.

"Mons." In order to save their left flank from being enveloped by the Germans under Von Kluck, the British and French Armies were forced to retire.

In the opening stages of the retreat the 1st Bn. Irish Guards acted as rear-guard to the 2nd Division.

Landrecies. The Battalion came under fire for the first time on August 23rd, and suffered five casualties. Two days later, at Landrecies, the Battalion, together with the 3rd Bn. Coldstream, beat off a heavy German night attack, the Battalion subsequently covering the Brigade's retirement from that town.

It was here that the big drum of the Battalion was captured by the Germans. It is to-day believed to be in the German War Museum in Berlin.

Le Cateau. The initial engagement of the British at Mons on August 23rd was followed by another successful rear-guard action at Le Cateau, fought by the Second Corps under General Sir Horace Smith-Dorrien.

Villers-Cotterêts. At Villers-Cotterêts on September 1st the Regiment and the Army suffered a great loss in the death of Lt.-Col. the Hon. G. H. Morris, commanding 1st Bn. Irish Guards.

Death of Lt.-Col. Hon. G. H. Morris. Colonel Morris, who had transferred from the Rifle Brigade into the Regiment on its formation, was born in Galway. He was the younger son of Lord Morris and Killanin, the famous Irish judge.

Recognised as one of the most brilliant staff officers in the Army, he long foresaw that war was inevitable and had spent his life qualifying himself in every way for higher command. He died as he would have wished, in the thick of the fight at the head of the Irishmen he loved so well.

Across the Somme, the Oise, the Aisne and the Marne the British Expeditionary Force had retired, until Spetember 5th, when the command to turn and counter-attack was given by General Joffre.

The story of the retreat is one that will live among the great traditions of the British Army. The battalions which took part were composed largely of reservists who had just been recalled from civil life; men whose feet were soft and whose shoulders were unaccustomed to the weight of a pack.

The retreat lasted thirteen days. It was one long drawn-out rear-guard action. The fighting took place along a line of about twenty-five miles and backwards for a distance of about eighty miles, which was covered by forced marches at night as well as by day.

Hardly for an hour were the British permitted any rest or respite. The actual distance covered on the map during the retreat was just over 170 miles. In actual fact many battalions marched considerably further. The Irish Guards being required on several occasions to march 20 and 25 miles during the day.

The heat was intense and marching was made extremely difficult owing to the congested state of the roads. The troops in all probability suffered as much hardship during this period as at any time during the war. The one thing that was never short was food, which says a great deal for the organisation of the supply services at this early stage of the war.

THE BATTLES OF THE MARNE AND THE AISNE.

On September 6th the advance of the Allied Armies began and the Marne was crossed three days later with little opposition.

The Allies now maintained their pressure on the retreating Germans, gradually forcing them back to the Aisne. The British were the first to cross that river on September 12th–13th. The Germans, however, now stiffened by fresh reinforcements, renewed their resistance, with the result that by September 15th there was a complete deadlock.

Boitron. The Irish Guards played their part in the Battle of the Marne, and at Boitron, on September 7th, captured a German Machine Gun Company.

"Marne, 1914." The Battalion crossed the Petit Morin river on September 8th.

The five days which followed prior to the crossing of the Aisne were most trying. This was partly due to the congestion of the traffic and the chaos in the villages that had been abandoned by the enemy.

"Aisne, 1914." The River Aisne was crossed at the Pont D'Arcy on September 14th. The Battalion then fought its way forward to the high ground above Soupir, where, for the first time, the men dug themselves in.

The Battle of the Marne ranks among the decisive battles of the world. It turned the tide of invasion and caused the German Armies to retreat ; at one time, indeed, the Armies of Von Kluck and Von Bulow were in actual jeopardy.

"THE RACE FOR THE SEA."

The immense stopping power of the rifle, the machine gun and the trench in defence now became apparent. The result of this was that neither side could make any headway by frontal attack. Both sides now endeavoured by pushing farther and farther north, to envelop the flank of their enemy.

The succession of movements resulting is now known as the "race for the sea" or the "race for the Channel ports."

The British Army was withdrawn from the Aisne, and the whole force began moving to Flanders in the first fortnight in October. This movement to the north, while it shortened considerably the lines of communication of the British Forces, imposed on them the most arduous task of defending the Channel ports; the capture of which, now that the capture of Paris was no longer possible, became the principal aim of the German Commanders.

"Ypres." The First Battle of Ypres followed and dragged on until the middle of November. During this period and up to the end of the battle the 1st Bn. Irish Guards was fighting almost continuously.

Klein Zillebeke. The Battalion was practically overwhelmed on November 1st, when after a terrific bombardment the Germans attacked Klein Zillebeke. It rallied, however, and was able to retire in good order.

Polygon Wood. On November 12th the 1st Bn. Irish Guards and 2nd Bn. Grenadier Guards were attached to and led the 1st Guards Brigade in a night attack near Polygon Wood. The Brigade was commanded by Brig.-General C. FitzClarence, V.C., who had only just vacated the appointment of Lieut.-Colonel Commanding the Irish Guards.

Death of Brig.-Gen. C. FitzClarence, V.C. During the attack General FitzClarence, "O.C., Menin Road," as he was affectionately called—was killed. His death was a serious loss to the Army, a brave and brilliant leader, whose quick decision at Gheluvelt on October 31st, when he ordered the Worcesters up from reserve, led to the re-capture of the village.

No single action in the war did more to save the Channel ports.

Brig.-General FitzClarence as recently as March, 1931, was described in a French newspaper ("Le Petit Calaisien") as the man who saved France and the Allied Cause.

To the staunchness and gallantry of the Irish Guards during the fighting round Ypres, the Brigadier, Lord Cavan*, commanding the 4th Guards Brigade, paid a striking tribute in a message he sent to the Battalion on November 20th. " I want you to convey to every man in your Battalion," he wrote to the Commanding Officer, " that I consider that the safety of the right flank of the British section depended entirely upon their staunchness after the disastrous day, November 1st. Those of them that were left made history, and I can never thank them enough for the way in which they recovered themselves, and showed the enemy that Irish Guards must be reckoned with, however hard hit."

Officially, the First Battle of Ypres ended on November 22nd, 1914. The British casualties were very heavy, the losses between October 14th and November 30th alone amounted to 58,000. Many battalions were now scarcely larger than platoons.

TRENCH WARFARE.

That winter saw the beginning of the long period of trench warfare. The principal characteristic of trench warfare is its deadly monotony and discomfort.

It soon became apparent, as knowledge of this form of warfare increased, that it was only highly disciplined troops who could endure long spells of trench warfare without deteriorating morally and physically. The training of the Brigade of Guards rendered them particularly suitable, and they soon began to excite the envy and admiration of the whole Army.

Cuinchy Brick-Stacks. At the end of January, 1915, the Brigade moved to the trenches at the so-called Cuinchy Brick-Stacks.

It was here on February 1st, and again on February 6th, that the Irish Guards delivered successful attacks against the enemy. In the action of February 1st the

* Afterwards General the Earl of Caven, K.P., G.C.B., G.C.M.G.. G.C.V.O., Colonel of the Irish Guards from 1925 to the present date.

L/Cpl. O'Leary, V.C. Regiment earned its first Victoria Cross, when L/Corporal O'Leary rushed two barricades alone and, single-handed, killed eight Germans and took two prisoners.

The casualties on this occasion were rather heavy, the Battalion losing 5 officers and 32 other ranks.

Neuve Chapelle. At the end of February the British made an attempt at piercing the German lines at Neuve Chapelle, a costly effort which yielded little result.

The Brigade was in Divisional reserve at this time, and took no actual part in the battle.

Soon after, on April 26th, there began the Second Battle of Ypres. This was the first occasion on which the Germans made use of a lethal (chlorine) gas. The use of this gas came as a complete surprise ; and our troops were not provided with proper anti-gas protection at this period.

The Germans came within an ace of gaining a great victory, but fortunately they were surprised by their own success and did not follow up their initial advantage.

The casualties due to the gas amongst the British and Canadian troops were very heavy.

"Festubert." On May 9th–16th was fought the indecisive action of Festubert.

La Cour d'Avoue. On May 15th the Battalion attacked the farm known as La Cour d'Avoue. Before the hour fixed for the advance the Battalion came under terrible machine gun fire. When at length the time came to move forward very little progress was possible. The losses were heavy, the Battalion losing 18 officers and 461 other ranks.

Formation of 2nd Bn. Irish Guards. On July 15th a Second Battalion of the Regiment was formed, and proceeded to France in August under the command of Lt.-Col. the Hon. L. Butler.

Formation of Guards Division. In August, 1915, the Guards Division was formed, and Major-General the Earl of Cavan became its first commander. It gave great pleasure to all Irish Guardsmen who had served under Lord Cavan in the 4th Guards Brigade, when their tried and trusted leader received his well-earned promotion.

The strength of the British Expeditionary Force was now being increased from day to day by the arrival of the New Army (Kitchener) Divisions.

Evacuation of Gallipoli. The evacuation of the Gallipoli Peninsula occurred about this time. This campaign had been brilliantly conceived and would have had a far reaching effect on the result of the war had it been successful.

The campaign failed from a variety of causes and resulted in very heavy casualties.

The original landing took place on St. George's Day, April 23rd, 1915.

The Australians and New Zealanders and the 29th Division gained immortal glory. The Leinsters, the Dublins and the Munsters, who formed part of the 29th Division, added many deeds of valour to their imperishable past.

Mesopotamia. Surrender of General Townsend. Another expedition was sent up the Persian Gulf to invade Mesopotamia. This ended in disaster when General Townsend and his whole force of 2,070 British troops and 6,000 Indians surrendered to the Turks at Kut-el-Amara.

The full story of the hardships endured by the troops that surrendered at Kut will never be known, but it forms one of the blackest pictures in the terrible annals of war.

General Sir Stanley Maude (Coldstream Guards) was subsequently sent out to take charge of the campaign in Mesopotamia.

Relief of Kut. He completely restored the situation, gaining a series of brilliant victories which culminated in the capture of Baghdad and the rout of the Turkish forces.

When at the very height of his fame General Maude died of cholera in Baghdad.

Bethune. To return to France, in September, 1915, a fresh attempt at piercing the German lines was now made at Bethune, with a view to assisting a great French offensive in Champagne.

"Loos." This brought about the Battle of Loos, where the 2nd Bn. Irish Guards received its baptism of fire on September 25th. The Battalion captured its objectives, and held the ground gained for three days.

Both Battalions subsequently held the section of the line in and about the Hohenzollern Redoubt, where they had many bombing encounters with the enemy.

Death of Colonel Madden. It was here that Lt.-Col. Madden, commanding the 1st Battalion, received the wounds from which he afterwards died.

Colonel Madden was born in Clones, Co. Monaghan. He transferred to the Irish Guards from the 3rd King's Own Hussars soon after the formation of the Regiment. Colonel Madden's death robbed the Regiment of the services of one of its most valued and experienced officers.

Laventie. In November the Guards Division took over a section of the line at Laventie, and forthwith set about improving the trenches in their accustomed manner.

The two Battalions of the Irish Guards stayed here engaged in trench warfare until February, 1916, when the Division went into reserve.

Death of Lord Desmond Fitz Gerald. As the result of a lamentable bombing accident, which occurred on the sands at Calais, Lord Desmond FitzGerald, Second-in-Command of the 1st Battalion, was killed, and Captain T. E. G. Nugent and Father Lane Fox were seriously wounded.

Lord Desmond FitzGerald was the second son of the 5th Duke of Leinster. He went out to France in 1914 as Adjutant of the 1st Battalion, and had quickly made his mark as a fine leader. A brave and gallant officer, who will never be forgotten by those who had the privilege of knowing him.

In March of that year the two Battalions were again at Ypres. The name of Ypres will long be held sacred by all Irish Guardsmen ; for, in defence of that City, which was France, the Regiment endured some of its greatest hardships and there perished some of the bravest and the best

THE SOMME.

The Germans now began an intensive attack against the French at Verdun, a fortress, the possession of which was recognised as of vital importance in the war on the Western Front.

In defence of that place the French had to exert their full strength.

Great as was the effort made by the French ; without the help of the Allies they could not have withstood the German onslaught.

"Somme." To relieve the pressure on the Verdun front, Sir Douglas Haig (who had succeeded Sir John French in command in December, 1915), in conjunction with the French, launched a direct attack against the Germans on the Somme front. This attack was supported by the greatest concentration of artillery that had yet been seen in the war.

Towards the end of July, the Guards Division moved from the Ypres Area to the Somme, and by the beginning of September was ready to take part in the battle.

The 'Quadrilateral.' On September 13th, the 2nd Battalion, then holding the trenches at Ginchy, was ordered to send a Company to take part in an attack on a German strong-point known as the "Quadrilateral." The artillery support was inadequate and No. 2 Company of the 2nd Battalion, after very heavy losses, had to return to their trenches. The Battalion lost 4 officers and 120 O.R.'s killed.

Ginchy. On September 15th the Guards Division delivered a great attack against the Ginchy Ridge. For the first time in the history of the Regiment, both Battalions of the Irish Guards went into action together, the 1st Battalion being commanded by Lt.-Col. R. C. McCalmont, and the 2nd Battalion by Lt.-Col. the Hon. L. Butler.

Although the enemy's resistance was desperate, and the Guards' casualties exceptionally severe, the ridge was carried and securely held.

On September 25th the Guards Division delivered a further attack, the 2nd Battalion being in reserve on this occasion. The 1st Battalion led the attack of the 1st Guards Brigade, and all objectives were taken.

Both Battalions received the thanks of their respective Brigadiers for the part they had played in the Somme fighting.

The attacks on the Somme had met with considerable success, but the casualties were very great on both sides.

Whether the victories of the Somme achieved all that is claimed for them is hard to say, but there can be no doubt the German Army never properly recovered from the great hardships endured during this period.

The victory helped to save Verdun, and it broke the spirit of the German Army, which had entered the battle at the zenith of its efficiency and enthusiasm.

A long period of trench warfare now followed, the Guards Division holding the line about Les Boeufs, Combles and Sailly-Saillisel.

The hands of the clock on the church tower at Sailly-Saillisel, which was destroyed by shell-fire, were brought home by an officer. They now serve as the hands of the clock in the Regimental Orderly Room.

The Guards Division spent a very hard winter, suffering considerably from the intense cold and the appalling condition of the ground, which months of the heaviest shell-fire had churned into a morass.

Both in work in the trenches and on field railways, both Battalions fully justified their reputation as the best digging Battalions of the British Army.

It is interesting to note that at this time Pipers joined the Battalions for the first time.

THE GERMAN WITHDRAWAL, 1917.

Mainly as a result of the Somme offensive the Germans withdrew from the Somme front to the Hindenburg Line, a distance of about 15 miles. This withdrawal came somewhat as a surprise to the Higher Command, and the plans for the next British offensive had to be altered considerably. Preparations for another offensive about Arras were begun.

The same attention to initial preparations was made as on the Somme; and the same early success was attained. The initial success failed to materialize, however, and the battle ended in heavy bombardments, followed by a series of advances on limited objectives.

Arras. Neither Battalions of the Regiment took part in the Battle of Arras.

Messines. After the Battle of Arras an attack on the Messines Ridge was undertaken.

The Battle of Messines was a triumph of forethought and careful organisation on the part of the commander,

General Sir H. Plumer. General Sir Herbert Plumer, and his Chief of Staff, Major-General C. Harington.* Complete success attended this effort, and there was a revival of spirit throughout the Armies in France.

During the Battle of Messines the Guards Division was in reserve and took no active part in the battle.

* Afterwards General Sir Charles Harington, G.B.E., K.C.B., D.S.O., who commanded the British Forces in Constantinople in 1922–1924, when the 1st Bn. Irish Guards were quartered there.

At this period the French Army was going through a very bad time, and some regiments actually mutinied.

Third Battle of Ypres.

Passhendaele.

In order to give the French time to restore the situation in their Army, the British Commander-in-Chief was forced to engage his troops in the series of battles on the Passhendaele Ridge. The battles extended over a period of nearly three months.

These operations achieved their object by drawing the German troops away from the French, but at a very great cost.

The weather again played an important part, the ground, drenched by the heavy rains, became a quagmire, and the tanks, on which so much hope was set, were unable to operate successfully.

It was during the battles of Passhendaele that the Regiment lost two officers who could ill be spared.

Death of Lt.-Col. E. B. Greer, M.C.

On July 27th, the Guards Division crossed the Yser Canal. During the attack on the first objective on July 31st, Lieut.-Col. Greer, commanding 2nd Battalion, was killed.

Colonel Greer, who was only 25, was one of a band of brilliant young officers whom the war was rapidly bringing to the front, when he was struck down on the threshold of his career. Great as were his military qualities, he will probably be best remembered in the Irish Guards as an athlete.

Death of Father Knapp, D.S.O., M.C.

On August 1st, Father Knapp, the Roman Catholic Priest to the 2nd Battalion, was killed.

Father Knapp was by no means a young man and when he joined the 2nd Battalion he at once endeared himself to all ranks by his great faith, courage and simplicity. He embodied all the christian virtues, sympathetic and brave almost to a fault.

Greatly as the Battalion mourned his loss, it was almost impossible to grieve for him, as never was mortal man more prepared to meet his end.

Sergeant Moyney, V.C. On September 13th the Germans made a determined attack on a number of posts which the 2nd Battalion was holding. It was on this occasion that Sergeant Moyney and L/Corporal Woodcock were awarded the Victoria Cross for splendid feats of endurance and courage.

Sergeant Moyney held a post against all attacks for 96 hours, and then fought his way back through the enemy to our line.

L/Cpl. Woodcock, V.C. Corporal Woodcock risked his life to go back and save a wounded comrade. He was killed six months later at Ayette, near Arras. Both Battalions took part in the attack across the Broembeek on October 9th.

"Cambrai." On November 27th came the Battle of Cambrai. Here the tanks were given full opportunity, and in the first days they proved their power. Unfortunately the indications of the coming of the great German counter-attack were not correctly appreciated, and the arrangements to meet it came too late to be thoroughly effective.

Bourlon Wood. In the bitter fighting about Cambrai the Irish Guards again played a prominent part. The 2nd Battalion, commanded by Lt.-Col. the Hon. H. R. L. G. Alexander, attacked and captured a portion of Bourlon Wood on November 27th, taking many prisoners. The Germans, however, counter-attacked in great force, and after a desperate hand-to-hand struggle the remnant of the Battalion fought its way back to the old line.

Gouzeaucourt. On November 30th, after the Germans had broken through at Gouzeaucourt, the 1st Guards Brigade counter-attacked.

The 2nd Bn. Grenadier Guards and the 1st Bn. Irish Guards, commanded by Lt.-Col. R. V. Pollok, led the attack, which was successful and resulted in the recapture of Gouzeaucourt and the Gonnelieu Ridge.

Gonnelieu. Five days later the Germans raided the trenches occupied by the 1st Battalion at Gonnelieu, and met with some success, the situation being restored by a most gallant counter-attack led by C.S.M. Usher.

THE GERMAN OFFENSIVE, MARCH, 1918.

By the beginning of 1918, Great Britain was faced with a serious situation.

The Russian Revolution had freed a million and a half of enemy troops, additional guns and much ammunition for use on the Western Front. The military assistance from the United States, who had come into the war on April 6th, 1917, still needed time to materialize.

The man-power of the British Armies was gradually becoming exhausted. The heavy casualties sustained by the infantry in the operations of the previous autumn, and the increasing difficulty of providing adequate reinforcements, led now to a reduction of the number of battalions in Infantry Brigades from four to three.

As a result of this reduction, the 4th Bn. Grenadier Guards, the 3rd Bn. Coldstream Guards and the 2nd Bn. Irish Guards were withdrawn from the Guards Division to form a new Brigade in the 31st Division.

The German objective now became the capture of Amiens, and the separation of the British and French Armies.

On March 21st the long expected storm broke and sixty-four German Divisions were hurled against the junction of the British and French Armies.

The Fifth (British) Army was almost overcome. The Allies were hard put to stem the German advance, but eventually this was achieved, and the Germans were checked almost within field-artillery range of Amiens.

The Germans then changed their objective and struck hard for the Channel ports. They failed in their efforts. Of those troops that helped to cause this failure the

1st Bn. and 2nd Bn. Irish Guards, who formed part of the Guards Division and 31st Division respectively, played an heroic part.

The 1st Battalion, south of Arras with the Guards Division, broke up the advance completely, suffering comparatively few casualties.

"Hazebrouck." The 2nd Battalion, after taking part in the withdrawal of the 31st Division, moved to the Hazebrouck area and took part in the defence of Nieppes Forest. It was here on April 13th that the Battalion played a prominent part in the heroic counter-attack of the composite Guards Brigade.

This was the 2nd Battalion's last hard fight. After this it took no more active part in the war, but remained at Criel Plage, near Dieppe, training young officers.

By July, 1918, a new line was established within 10 miles of Amiens, and on this line the battle was stabilised.

Maréchal Foch, who had become Generalissimo of the Allied Forces, could now look with equanimity on the situation.

After the German offensive in March and April no further attack on so great a scale was made by the enemy on the British front. On the French front, however, the Germans made two more great attacks; the first at the end of May in Champagne; and the second early in July between Chateau Thierry and the Argonne. On each occasion, after initial successes, the enemy was eventually repulsed.

It now became apparent that the enemy's offensive spirit was at last exhausted, and thereafter every attempt to attain his main objective failed.

THE ADVANCE TO VICTORY, AUGUST 1918.

The British participation in the combined Allied offensive, which continued without pause until the Armistice, commenced on August 8th.

The Fourth British Army attacked in conjunction with the French First Army east and south-east of Amiens. It was not until a fortnight later, however, that the Guards Division took part in the battle.

The offensive was immediately followed by a series of successes.

On August 21st the Guards Division, as part of the Third Army, took part in the attack which was to be pushed on indefinitely.

From this time on the 1st Battalion (now commanded by Lt.-Col. R. R. C. Baggallay) played a prominent part in all the big attacks in which the Division took part.

"Hindenburg Line." The Battalion's share at the breaking of the Hindenburg Line was on September 27th, when the Battalion attacked and crossed the Canal du Nord.

On November 4th what proved to be the final advance was commenced, the objective of the Guards Division being Maubeuge.

Palestine. Meanwhile in Palestine General Allenby had been preparing for his final overthrow of the Turks.

During the early summer the progressive deterioration of the morale and fighting power of the Turks had been most marked. This was evidenced by many signs of which the increasing number of deserters to the British lines was the most apparent.

On October 1st, 1918, General Allenby occupied Damascus, and finally, by the conquest of Aleppo, cut off the Turks in Mesopotamia from their base.

Salonica. The Salonica Force, which during 1917 and the beginning of 1918 had made no further attempts to break the Bulgarian line, now turned to the offensive.

On the 14th September the combined Allied offensive began. It met with complete success, and the Bulgar Army retreated in confusion.

That same month Bulgaria and Turkey laid down their arms.

Italy. In Italy the Allies turned at length from defence to attack, and drove the Austrians back over their own frontiers.

The British Fourteenth Corps during these operations was commanded by General the Earl of Cavan.

The surrender of Bulgaria and Turkey now made Austria unable to hold her own in the Balkans, and on November 3rd an armistice was declared.

With the United States now on the side of the Allies, Germany was left alone to fight the world in arms.

By November 9th the Guards Division had entered Maubeuge, the Canadians were in Mons and the Second Army had crossed the Scheldt.

The whole of the British line had now passed from France into Belgium.

Collapse of Germany. Faced with the insoluable problem of evacuating what remained to them of Northern France and Belgium, the German Supreme Command made overtures to Maréchal Foch for an armistice.

Germany was in the throes of political revolution, and its Royal representatives had already abdicated.

The Germany Army was no longer controllable as a military organisation, its retreat threatened to become a chaotic struggle to move. The pressure of the Allied Armies would soon confine still further the already seething area in which the masses of defeated troops were hastening eastwards.

On November 10th Maréchal Foch received the German delegates.

The Armistice. The Armistice was signed at 10 p.m. that night and hostilities ceased at 11 a.m. next morning, November 11th, 1918.

"Just before 11 a.m. all batteries opened fire. Each gunner was determined to be the last man to fire a shot at the Germans. And then, in the midst of the rolling thunder of rapid fire, the teams straining every nerve to throw the last shell into the breech of their guns before the 'Cease fire' sounded, eleven o'clock struck, the first blast of the bugles pierced the air and, with the last note, silence reigned."

. . . . .

There is always a danger that in attempting to follow the fortunes of a regiment throughout its history, the relationship which the effort of that particular regiment bears to the whole is lost sight of.

The effort made by the Irish Guards in the Great War will bear comparison with that of any unit in the Army.

The strength of the Regiment in August, 1914, was 997. There were borne on the strength of the Irish Guards during the Great War 293 officers and 9,340 other ranks, of which 115 officers and 2,235 other ranks were killed or died of wounds ; 195 officers, 5,541 other ranks were wounded. The number of prisoners for both Battalions was 246.

The awards for gallantry made to individuals include 3 Victoria Crosses, 14 Distinguished Service Orders, 67 Military Crosses, 77 Distinguished Conduct Medals, 244 Military Medals, besides many other foreign decorations.

The war of 1914–1918 was unlike any war previously waged by Great Britain, who, in all her former wars, had relied upon the professional Army, augmented to a greater or lesser degree by volunteers. In this war, not only was the whole population of Great Britain involved, but the whole population of the Empire.

In January, 1916, conscription had to be resorted to.

The British Forces in the field, including Dominion, Colonial, and Indian and Native Troops, at one time amounted to 5,500,000. The total casualties in the war amounted to over 3,000,000.

At one time the war was costing 7½ million pounds per day.

These figures, astonishing as they are, can give no true picture of the immensity of the effort made to support these vast forces in the field, and to provide them with all the various requirements of an Army.

. . . . .

Conclusion In conclusion, it is only fitting that a short account should be given of the character and career of that great man, Field Marshal Earl Haig.

As Commander-in-Chief of the British Armies in France from December 22nd, 1915, to the end of the war, he bore the greatest responsibility that has ever been placed on the shoulders of any British Commander in the field.

Lord Haig was born in 1861, and was therefore 54 when he assumed command of the British Expeditionary Force.

He joined the 7th Hussars from Oxford University in 1885, and subsequently commanded the 17th Lancers from 1901–1903.

It is interesting to note that one of the first occasions on which he came into prominence in military circles was when acting as a Junior Staff Officer to the late Major-General Sir Hugh McCalmont on manœuvres in Southern Ireland in August, 1899.

He still further enhanced his military reputation during the South African War, when he acted as Staff Officer to Major-General Sir John French, afterwards Field Marshal The Earl of Ypres.

He rose rapidly to General's rank, being appointed Major-General in 1904 at the age of 43.

The size of modern armies is so vast that it is impossible for a commander to be known to his troops as in former days.

Lord Haig had to endure much criticism. He remained steadfast throughout it all and refused to be distracted from his object, the ultimate defeat of the German Armies.

Ready at all times to subordinate his personal ambition for the good of the cause, he would never agree or be party to any plan which he thought would unnecessarily jeopardize the safety of those under his command.

One of the greatest tragedies of any war is its aftermath.

So many men have had their lives completely disorganised, that when the war is over it is difficult for them to settle down in civil life and resume their normal occupations.

Lord Haig never forgot or lost faith in those who had served him so well, and who had rendered possible the great victories of the British Army.

As founder and moving spirit of the British Legion, he spent the rest of his life in espousing their cause.

He died at the age of 68, a great soldier and a great gentleman who never forsook a comrade.

CHAPTER VII.

From the Armistice to the Present Day.

When at 11 a.m. on November 11th, 1918, Commanding Officers announced the Armistice to their respective units, the news was received with the dignity and self-control which had marked the British soldier from the beginning to the end of the war.

Officers and men went quietly about their ordinary duties, scarcely realizing at first that the end had come and that the long strain was over.

Out of the 81 days which had elapsed since August 21st the Guards Division had spent 54 in the line, and 29 of these had been actual days of hard fighting.

The days at Maubeuge passed pleasantly for the Battalion. The town was practically undamaged, and the inhabitants vied with one another in their kindness and hospitality towards their deliverers.

Every trace of the wear and tear of the recent fighting and of the long and muddy marches was speedily removed. In a very short time the Battalion resumed its customary parade-ground appearance.

On November 14th a Thanksgiving Service was held in Maubeuge Cathedral, the Battalion finding the Guard of Honour.

The March to Cologne. The 2nd Battalion, which had been at Criel Plage, and the remnants of the 4th Guards Brigade, rejoined the Division on November 17th.

On November 18th the Division started to march forward with the British Army into Germany. This march was an arduous one, carried out in extremely wet weather, over roads ankle deep in mud.

Occasionally billets were hard to find and the question of supplies was always a difficult one. The head of the Division crossed the frontier on December 11th and marched to Cologne, where it formed part of the Garrison.

Cologne. The 2nd Battalion was quartered in the Pioneer Barracks; fitted with every luxury, from electric light to drying rooms and baths, and the 1st Bn. was quartered in two school buildings. Both Battalions remained in Cologne until March 1919, when the Guards' Division returned to England and marched triumphantly through the streets of London.

Demobilisation. With the Armistice came a re-action, bringing with it the desire for immediate demobilisation and a return to civil occupation. Unfortunately, the civilian labour market was unable to absorb all the ex-soldiers, many of whom had had their lives disorganised by military service and were unable to settle down to their former work; much disappointment and distress ensued, which exists even to the present day. There was, at this time, a very natural desire amongst the men themselves to get out of the Army as quickly as possible. It was also necessary for financial reasons that the Army should be reduced to its peace time strength. Many units of all arms had to be disbanded.

The 2nd Bn. Disbanded. On March 31st, 1919, the 2nd Battalion Irish Guards was disbanded and its Colours, which had only been presented by His Royal Highness the Prince of Wales, in Cologne on January 14th, were laid up in the Roman Catholic Church at Caterham. The 1st Battalion, now stationed at Warley, once more resumed its peace-time duties.

The Russian Relief Force. In May, 1918, a landing of Allied troops was made at Murmansk in Northern Russia.

This landing was made at the invitation of the Soviet Government owing to the German and Finnish threat to seize the ports of Murmansk and Petchenja.

Soon after the Allied troops had landed the attitude of the Soviet Government became decidedly hostile. The local population, however, welcomed the presence of the Allied troops, and unanimously decided to defend

Murmansk against the Germans with the co-operation of the Allies, thereby disobeying the orders of the Central Society.

Offensive operations against the Germans then commenced. The rapid approach of the Armistice, however, altered matters, and a large proportion of the German troops were withdrawn.

As the winter drew on the Bolshevik efforts to turn the Allies out of Archangel and Murmansk became stronger and stronger. A relief force was then sent out to Russia, under General Rawlinson. An appeal for volunteers to serve with this Force met with great response.

Many Irish Guardsmen volunteered, and two officers of the Regiment lost their lives, Lieutenant J. C. Zigomala was accidentally killed and Lieutenant Lord Settrington, the eldest son of Lieut.-Colonel the Earl of March,* was killed in action.

During March and April, 1919, the Allies were successful in breaking up the final Bolshevik attacks with great loss.

It had already been decided to evacuate Russia, but, owing to Archangel and Murmansk being ice-bound, the evacuation did not take place until October, 1920.

On July 22nd, 1920, the Brigade of Guards and the Household Cavalry resumed their full dress. During the war and up to this date the King's Guard and all duties had mounted in service dress. The first occasion on which the Irish Guards wore full dress after the war was on St. Patrick's Day, 1921. This was also the first occasion on which the Pipers had ever worn full dress.

Return to Full Dress.

The Coal Strike.

On April 5th, 1921, the Coal Strike broke out. The Battalion was moved from Aldershot to Kensington Gardens, where it remained until the close of the Strike. On this occasion a General Mobilisation was ordered, and 11 Officers and 88 Reservists re-joined from the Reserve.

* The present Duke of Richmond and Gordon.

Foreign Service. On March 3rd, 1922, orders were received for the Battalion, which was at Windsor, to be held in readiness to embark for Constantinople. Embarkation furlough was granted to all, with the result that the customary St. Patrick's Day celebrations were abandoned for that year. On Friday, April 21st, His Majesty the King inspected the Battalion at Windsor, and four days later the Battalion was inspected by the Colonel of the Regiment Field Marshal the Earl of Ypres. Immediately after the inspection, the Battalion marched out of Victoria Barracks and entrained for Southampton. That night the Battalion embarked on "H.M.S. Derbyshire."

Arrival in Constantinople. The Battalion arrived in Constantinople on May 12th, 1922. The Irish Guards were sent to Turkey to form part of the garrison in Constantinople.

In order to understand the situation in Turkey at this time it is necessary to go back a few years. The Turkish Armies were completely destroyed in 1918 by General Allenby's great victories in Palestine. The Turks signed an Armistice at Mudros on October 30th, 1918. The Allies, however, were far too busy making peace to think of Turkey, and eventually, when in August, 1920, the Treaty of Sèvres was signed, it was so harsh that the Turks refused to ratify it.

Events in Turkey. War weary as the Turks were, they were roused to action by the great Nationalist leader, Mustapha Kemal, and, after suffering several defeats, they finally rallied and drove the Greek armies out of Anatolia. The Greek Army had landed at Smyrna in 1919, nominally in support of the Allied cause, and to force the Turks to ratify the Treaty of Sèvres. The French at once withdrew all their troops in the area, and left the small British force at Chanak and Ishmid to face the Turkish forces alone.

It was at this critical period that the 1st Guards' Brigade was sent out from Aldershot to take over the duties of garrison at Constantinople. On arrival at that place, the 1st Guards' Brigade was joined by the 1st Battalion, Irish Guards, who had been having a very anxious time facing the Turks at Ishmid on the Bosphorous.

Eventually a convention was signed at Mudania on October 11th, 1922, and matters quietened down. Peace was finally concluded at Lausanne on July 24th, 1923, the Turks getting practically everything they asked for.

While in Constantinople the Battalion took part in the ceremony of Trooping the Colour in 1922 and 1923, the Battalion finding the Escort on both occasions. On September 1st, 1923, Lieutenant-General Sir Charles Harrington, the General Officer Commanding-in-Chief, British Forces in Turkey, made his farewell inspection of the Battalion. On September 5th, the Battalion embarked on " H.M.T. Egypt " en route for Gibraltar. The Lieutenant-Colonel Commanding the Regiment received the following extract from a telegram dispatched by the Commander-in-Chief to the Earl of Cavan, Chief of the Imperial General Staff :—

> " Irish Guards created great impression by their march through Constantinople this morning, in perfect order, to embark, preceded by the Massed Drums of the Brigade of Guards."

Gibraltar. The Battalion arrived in Gibraltar on September 13th. On September 18th the Battalion found a Guard of Honour for the arrival in Gibraltar of His Excellency General Sir Charles Monro, Governor and Commander-in-Chief. The Battalion remained in Gibraltar until April 4th, 1924, when it returned to England on " H.M.T. Glengorm Castle," arriving at Southampton on April 9th.

Arrival Home. From Southampton the Battalion entrained for Woking and went into quarters at Inkerman Barracks. The following telegram was received from His Majesty the King :—

> " As your Colonel-in-Chief, I wish all ranks a happy return to their homes and families after two years of

foreign service. I have heard from General Harrington how splendidly the Battalion has upheld the traditions of the Brigade of Guards while at Constantinople."

"Guardsman." In June, 1923, an Army Order was issued which gave official sanction to the use of the designation of "Guardsman." Hitherto the designation of "Private" had been used. In October, 1924, Regimental Headquarters were moved from Buckingham Gate to Birdcage Walk.

The building vacated at Buckingham Gate was first occupied on December 12th, 1901, and prior to that date Regimental Headquarters had been at the Horse Guards.

The Death of F. M. the Earl of Ypres. The death of the Colonel of the Regiment, Field Marshal the Earl of Ypres, much to the regret of all ranks, occurred on May 22nd, 1925. The funeral took place on May 26th from Westminster Abbey. An Escort and Bearer Party was detailed from the Battalion.

Gen. the Earl of Cavan, Fourth Colonel of the Regt. General The Earl of Cavan was appointed Colonel of the Regiment on May 23rd, 1925.

The Battalion, now stationed at Aldershot, took part in lining the streets on the occasion of the funeral of Her Majesty Queen Alexandra on Friday, November 27th, 1925.

The General Strike. On May 3rd, 1926, a General Strike occurred. The Battalion, which was engaged in Annual Musketry at Cowshott Camp, was immediately marched to Aldershot, where, that night with the remainder of the 1st Guards' Brigade, it proceeded in lorries to Victoria Park, London. From Victoria Park the Battalion was moved to the West India Docks, where it remained until the close of the Strike.

Unveiling of the Kitchener and Guard's Division Memorials.

A Guard of Honour was found by the Battalion at the unveiling of Lord Kitchener's Memorial on June 9th, 1926*, and the Battalion also took part in the ceremony of unveiling the Guards' Division Memorial by Field Marshal His Royal Highness the Duke of Connaught on October 16th.

Presentation of Colours 1927.

His Majesty the King presented Colours to the Battalion in the gardens of Buckingham Palace on May 28th, 1927.

The ceremony was to have taken place at Rushmoor Arena, Aldershot, in 1926, but, owing to the General Strike, it was postponed until this date. The Battalion was under the command of Lieutenant-Colonel R. V. Pollok, C.B.E., D.S.O. After the ceremony His Majesty addressed the Battalion :

"Fourteen years ago," he said, I gave you new Colours. You were a young Regiment then and the Colours bore no Honours upon them. Fourteen months later you were earning your first Honour in the Retreat from Mons. Let it be remembered that a retreat is the supreme trial of discipline and endurance in a soldier ; for those who can pass brilliantly through that trial will not be found wanting in the day of attack.

"I am not going to recount all your services, but only mention three names—Ypres 1914, Somme 1916, Cambrai 1917. In the first you showed that no losses and no perils could undermine your steadfastness even if you could not retaliate ; in the two last the sting and persistence of your attack evoked the admiration even of your enemies. Irish Guards—a Regiment which has fought through the Great War from beginning to end, is no longer a new Regiment. If you have not the names of Marlborough's and Wellington's victories on your Colours, as have your older companions in the Brigade of Guards, you have stood by their side and borne

* Field Marshal Lord Kitchener, Colonel of the Irish Guards, lost his life on June 5th, 1916, when the battleship in which he was travelling to Russia, struck a mine in the North Sea.

yourselves worthily of them in the fiercest and most stubborn contest in Military history. You have made a great beginning ; go on and prosper.

" I can count on you to take such prizes as may be won in peace ; and if, which God forbid, war should come, I know that you will maintain the honour of the Household Brigade and of the Irish Guards.

" With all confidence, I commit these Colours to your keeping."

The old Colours were laid-up in the Guards' Chapel by Lieut.-Colonel R. V. Pollok, C.B.E., D.S.O., commanding 1st Bn. Irish Guards on March 18th, 1928.

. . . . .

It is a habit in some quarters nowadays to picture the soldier as a fire-eater who thinks of nothing but killing and destruction ; a strike-breaker, a black-leg, ready at any time to deprive his fellow workers of their just dues.

How different is the reality. A soldier is a citizen of the country, a State servant, whose duty it is to carry out the orders of the State as represented by the Government of the day.

At the head of the State is His Majesty the King, to whom the soldier swears allegiance.

The tasks that a soldier may be called upon to perform either in peace or in war may frequently be distasteful to him personally, but that must not matter. A soldier is bound by his oath to serve his King, as head of the State, and to carry out the orders of His Majesty's Government, however difficult and unpleasant those orders may be.

The military profession is just as noble and as honourable as it ever was.

By maintaining a highly trained and efficient army a nation is not inciting others to make war, but is insuring against it. There can be no better insurance, provided that Army is animated by the high ideals of love of country, duty, loyalty and self-sacrifice.

THE END.

APPENDIX A.

BATTLE HONOURS.

"Mons."
"RETREAT FROM MONS," (Aug. 23rd).
"MARNE," 1914, (Sept. 8th).
"AISNE, 1914," (Sept. 14th).
"YPRES, 1914, '17," (Oct. 9th).
"Langemarck, 1914."
"Gheluvelt."
"Nonne Bosschen."
"FESTUBERT, 1915," (May 18th).
"LOOS" (Sept. 27th).
"SOMME, 1916, '18" (Sept. 15th).
"Flers-Courcelette."
"Morval."
"Pilckem."
"Poelcappelle."
"Passchendaele."
"CAMBRAI, 1917, '18" (Nov. 27th).
"St. Quentin."
"Lys."
"HAZEBROUCK" (April 13th).
"Albert, 1918."
"Bapaume, 1918."
"Arras, 1918."
"Scarpe, 1918."
"Drocourt-Queant."
"HINDENBURG LINE (Sept. 27th).
"Canal du Nord."
"Selle."
"Sambre."
"France and Flanders, 1914–18."

NOTE.

The Battle Honours in block letters are those borne on the Colours. The Colours are "decked" with a laurel wreath on the dates appearing in brackets.

APPENDIX B.

A short history of the lives and careers of the Colonels of the Regiment since its formation.

Field Marshal the Right Hon. the Earl Roberts of Kandahar and Pretoria, and of the City of Waterford, V.C., K.G., K.P., P.C., G.C.B., O.M., G.C.S.I., G.C.I.E.

Colonel of the Irish Guards from October 17th, 1900, until November 14th, 1914.

Frederick Sleigh Roberts was born at Cawnpore on September 30th, 1832.

His father, General Abraham Roberts, descended from a family long settled in County Waterford, was at that time commanding the Bengal European regiment, afterwards known as the Munster Fusiliers.

At the age of thirteen, Frederick Roberts was sent to Eton for a year, and in January, 1847, he entered the Royal Military College.

In 1851 he obtained his first commission in the Bengal Artillery; a few years later he transferred to the Bengal Horse Artillery. During his first term of service in India he was stationed at Peshawar, and while doing the normal duty of a battery officer he also acted as aide-de-camp to his father.

During the Indian Mutiny (1857) Roberts was present at the siege of Delhi, and was afterwards specially selected by General Sir Colin Campbell to act as guide to General Havelock's force, which subsequently relieved Sir Henry Lawrence and the garrison, who were besieged in the Residency at Lucknow. After the siege of Lucknow he was attached to a cavalry Brigade, and it was at Khudaganj in January, 1858, that he won his Victoria Cross. At great personal risk, he saved the life of a loyal Indian soldier who was being attacked by some mutineers; later in the day, under particularly gallant circumstances, he set a fine example by re-capturing, single-handed, a standard from the mutineers.

Roberts served in the Abyssinian Expedition of 1868, and the Lushai Expedition of 1871-2 ; in both these expeditions he greatly distinguished himself.

In January, 1875, he was made a Companion of the Bath and was promoted Brevet-Colonel. Three years later he was appointed to the command of the Punjaub Frontier Force.

In November of 1878 trouble started with the Afghans, and Colonel Roberts led one of three expeditions against them.

That year, at the age of 46, Colonel Roberts was promoted Major-General and was made a Knight Commander of the Bath.

In September, 1879, war broke out in Afghanistan and Sir Frederick Roberts advanced with a small force on Kabul, which city he entered after defeating the Afghans at Charasia.

In 1880 he made his famous march of 313 miles in 22 days to the relief of Kandahar in Afghanistan. For his services he was made a Grand Commander of the Bath and was appointed to the command of the Madras Army, but his health had suffered so much by his long service in India that he was compelled to return to England before he could take up the appointment.

Soon after he returned again to India, this time to become Commander-in-Chief.

In 1892 Sir Frederick Roberts returned to England and was raised to the Peerage. He was promoted Field Marshal in 1895 and became Commander-in-Chief in Ireland.

At the outbreak of the South African War in 1899 Lord Roberts was not given a command, as he was considered too senior.

The situation, however, became so serious that he eventually had to be sent out to take over the duties of Commander-in-Chief.

Soon after his arrival he defeated the Boers under Cronje at Paardeburg, and, continuing his advance, finally entered Pretoria, the capital of the Transvaal.

The Transvaal was then annexed, and Lord Roberts returned to England to receive the personal thanks of Queen Victoria. He was rewarded by the Queen with an Earldom and the Order of the Garter.

On the formation of the Irish Guards in 1900, Lord Roberts was appointed the first Colonel.

In 1903 he officially retired from his appointment as Commander-in-Chief, and at the same time King Edward VII publicly expressed his thanks to the Field Marshal for his services of over 50 years in India, Africa and at home. "During that period," His Majesty wrote, "you have performed every duty entrusted to you with unswerving zeal and unfailing success."

Lord Roberts was one of those who foresaw that war with Germany was inevitable, and that when it came our small Army would be unable to compete against the conscript Armies of Europe for any length of time.

He spent the years from 1903 to 1914 in trying to impress on his fellow countrymen the need for compulsory service. Although he failed in his task, he did much to arouse the interest of the nation in military matters.

When the Great War came Lord Roberts was as vigorous and as resolute as ever, although, by reason of his years, he was unable to take an active part.

He died on November 14th, 1914, while on a visit to The Expeditionary Force in France, where he had gone to welcome the Indian Troops on their arrival.

Field Marshal the Right Hon. the Earl Kitchener of Khartoum and of Broome, K.G., K.P., P.C., G.C.B., O.M., G.C.S.I., G.C.M.G., G.C.I.E.

Colonel of the Irish Guards from November 15th, 1914, until June 5th, 1916.

Horatio Herbert Kitchener was born at Gunsborough House, near Listowel in County Kerry, on June 24th, 1850.

He entered the Royal Military Academy at Woolwich in 1868, and obtained a commission in the Royal Engineers in January, 1871.

His first acquaintance with the East, with which he was to become so familiar, was in 1874, when he accompanied an expedition for surveying that part of Western Palestine which still remained unmapped.

Realising that trouble was brewing in Egypt, he managed to be at Alexandria on leave at the time of Arabi's revolt. He served through the campaign of 1882 and, thanks largely to his knowledge of Arabic, became second-in-command of the Egyptian Cavalry, when Sir Evelyn Wood was made Sirdar of the Egyptian Army.

During the Sudan War of 1881–1885, Kitchener commanded the column which was sent to relieve General Gordon at Khartoum.

In 1885 he was promoted Lieutenant-Colonel, and in 1886 took part in the Suakin campaign, in which he was seriously wounded. In June, 1888, he became Colonel and A.D.C. to Her Majesty Queen Victoria, who had formed a high and just estimate of Kitchener's talents.

In 1892 he succeeded Sir Francis Grenfell as Sirdar in Egypt, and was made Knight Commander of the Order of Saint Michael and Saint George. Lord Kitchener now set about organising the Egyptian Army and collecting the materials which were to render possible the great victories of the Sudan.

He was promoted Major-General in 1896, at the age of 46.

In the second Sudan War of 1896–1898 Sir Herbert Kitchener commanded the expedition that advanced up the Nile to Khartoum.

He defeated the Dervishes at Atbara and again at Omdurman. After this Great Britain assumed joint sovereignty with Egypt over the Sudan. Kitchener now returned home and was raised to the peerage, taking the title of Lord Kitchener of Khartoum.

When Lord Roberts was appointed Commander-in-Chief during the South African War, Lord Kitchener accompanied him as Chief of Staff, and served in this capacity until Lord Roberts returned home. During the last two years of the war Lord Kitchener was in command, and he eventually brought the war to a successful issue.

At the end of the war Lord Kitchener returned to England, but was almost immediately appointed Commander-in-Chief in India. During his command in India he reorganised the Indian Army, and was responsible for many improvements.

On returning home in 1909 Lord Kitchener was made a Field Marshal and received the Order of Saint Patrick.

In 1911 he was appointed Consul General in Egypt.

While in Egypt Lord Kitchener introduced many reforms both political and social, and he was responsible for the drainage system in the Nile Delta, which has added so much to the economic prosperity of the country.

At the outbreak of the war in August, 1914, Kitchener was appointed Secretary of State for War. It was entirely due to his energy and ability that a new army of 100,000 men was raised in an extremely short time. This army came to be known as " Kitchener's Army."

There was no man in whom the country had more confidence than Lord Kitchener, and his untimely death in 1916 came as a great shock to the whole nation.

He met his death when H.M.S. " Hampshire," on which he was travelling to Russia, was sunk by a mine in the North Sea.

Lord Kitchener became Colonel of the Irish Guards on the death of Lord Roberts in 1914.

Field Marshal Right Hon. the Earl of Ypres and High Lake, K.P., P.C., G.C.B., O.M., G.C.V.O., K.C.M.G.

Colonel, Irish Guards from June 6th, 1916, until May 22nd, 1925.

John Denton Pinkstone French was born on September 28th, 1852.

His father, who was in the Navy, belonged to the family of French, of Frenchpark, County Roscommon.

Losing both his parents during childhood, John French's early education was superintended by one of his sisters. After a short sojourn at a preparatory school he was sent to Eastman's Naval Academy at Portsmouth, where many naval officers have been educated. In 1866 he joined " H.M.S. Britannia " as a naval cadet. Thence he entered the Royal Navy, in which he remained altogether four years. The naval service, however, attracted him but little, and he decided to abandon it for the Army.

With this object in view he entered the Militia and on February 28th, 1874, obtained his first commission in the 8th Hussars, being transferred a few weeks later to the 19th Hussars. In this Regiment he served through every rank until he eventually gained Command.

His first experience of war was in the Sudan Expedition of 1884–1885, when he commanded a squadron of the 19th Hussars. During this campaign he gained high approbation for his conduct and resource. In 1888 he obtained command of the 19th Hussars and in 1891 took the Regiment to India.

After his period of Command had finished, Colonel French held various Staff appointments. In May, 1897, he received command of the 2nd Cavalry Brigade, and in 1899 he was transferred to the 1st Cavalry Brigade at Aldershot. The outbreak of the South African War thus offered him a unique opportunity of achieving a reputation as a cavalry officer. On September 23rd, 1899, he was appointed to command the mounted troops in Natal under Sir George White.

Throughout the campaign French greatly distinguished himself as a cavalry leader.

In 1899, at the age of 47, he was promoted Major-General and received the K.C.B. From South Africa Sir John French returned home to assume the command at Aldershot, which appointment he held until 1907. He was appointed Chief of the Imperial General Staff in 1912, and was promoted Field Marshal in 1913. In view of his previous record, Sir John French's selection to command the Expeditionary Force in August, 1914, was a foregone conclusion.

His period in command of the British Expeditionary Force was an extremely difficult one. First came the

Retreat from Mons, the battles of the Marne and the Aisne, and then the fighting round Ypres.

On December 22nd, 1915, Sir John was succeeded by Sir Douglas Haig, who had served on his Staff in South Africa. When he returned to England he was raised to the Peerage, taking the title of Viscount French of Ypres and High Lake, Co. Roscommon. Lord French was now entrusted to the command of the entire Forces in the United Kingdom. The remaining years of the war saw him busily employed until May, 1918, when he assumed the office of Lord Lieutenant of Ireland. Lord French held this appointment until 1921 and was raised to an Earldom, taking the title of Earl of Ypres.

Amongst many other honours he received the Order of Merit and Order of Saint Patrick. As well as being Colonel of the Irish Guards, he was Colonel of the 19th Hussars and Colonel-in-Chief of the Royal Irish Regiment.

Lord French died at Dover Castle on May 22nd, 1925, aged 75.

General the Earl of Cavan, K.P., G.C.B., G.C.M.G., G.C.V.O., G.B.E.

(The present Colonel of the Irish Guards.)

Lord Cavan was born at Ayot St. Lawrence, Herts, in 1865. The family of Lambart, to which Lord Cavan belongs, first went to Ireland in 1580. Sir Oliver Lambart, afterwards Lord Lambart, Baron of Cavan, defeated the famous Rory O'More and built the Fort at Galway in 1602. For his services in Ireland Lord Lambart was granted lands in the County Cavan by Queen Elizabeth.

Lord Cavan joined the Grenadier Guards in 1885 from the Royal Military College. His whole service was spent in the Grenadier Guards and he saw service with that Regiment in South Africa. In 1908 he was appointed to the command of the 1st Battalion.

When the Great War broke out Lord Cavan was on the Reserve of Officers, and was appointed to command the 2nd London Infantry Brigade (now the 168th

Brigade), afterwards commanding the 4th Guards Brigade.

In 1915 he was promoted Major-General and was appointed to the command of the Guards' Division on its formation. In 1916 he was promoted to command the XIV Corps. This corps was sent to Italy in 1917 in order to help restore the situation after the disastrous reverse suffered by the Italians at Caporetto. Lord Cavan was afterwards Commander-in-Chief of the British Forces in Italy and commanded the Xth Italian Army at the final victory of Vittoria Veneto.

From 1920–1922 he was General Officer Commanding at Aldershot and was made an Aide-de-Camp General to the King. He was promoted General in 1921. In 1921 he represented the War Office at the Disarmament Conference in Washington. Lord Cavan became Chief of the Imperial General Staff in 1922 and was appointed Colonel of the Irish Guards on the death of Field Marshal the Earl of Ypres in 1925. When his appointment as Chief of the Imperial General Staff terminated, Lord Cavan retired from the Active List of the Army.

He was made Captain of the Honourable Corps of Gentlemen-at-Arms in 1929.

APPENDIX C.

THE ORIGINAL GAZETTE DATED 1st MAY, 1900.

London Gazette.

1*st May*, 1900.

IRISH GUARDS.—Major Richard R. J. Cooper from Grenadier Guards to be Lieut.-Colonel, dated May 2nd, 1900.

The undermentioned officers to be Majors, dated May 2nd, 1900 :—

Major Douglas J. Hamilton from the Royal Fusiliers (City of London Regiment).

Captain George C. Nugent from Grenadier Guards.

*Captain and Brevet-Major Cecil F. Vandeleur, D.S.O., from Scots Guards, to be Captain, dated 2nd May, 1900.

Captain and Brevet-Major Cecil F. Vandeleur, D.S.O., is seconded for Special Service in South Africa. Dated 2nd May, 1900.

The undermentioned Officers to be Lieuts., dated May 2nd, 1900 :—

Lieut. Henry W. E. Earl of Kerry, from Grenadier Guards.

†Lieut. William E. Lord Oxmantown, from Coldstream Guards.

‡Lieut. Henry W. E. Earl of Kerry is seconded for service on the Staff, dated May 2nd, 1900.

* Major Vandeleur was killed in action in South Africa on August 31st, 1901, shortly after he was gazetted to the Regiment.

† Afterwards the Earl of Rosse.

‡ The present Marquis of Lansdowne.

APPENDIX D.

Lieutenant-Colonels Commanding the Regiment since the formation :

	From.	To.
Colonel V. J. Dawson, C.V.O... ..	1900	1905
Colonel R. J. Cooper, M.V.O. ..	1905	1909
Colonel G. C. Nugent, M.V.O. ..	1909	1913
Colonel C. FitzClarence, V.C.	1913	1914
Colonel D. J. Proby	1914	1917
*Colonel R. Le N. Lord Ardee, C.B...	1917	1918
Colonel Sir J. R. Hall, Bt., C.B.E. ..	1918	1919
Colonel R. C. A. McCalmont, D.S.O...	1919	1924
Colonel W. H. V. Darell, C.M.G., D.S.O.	1924	1928
Colonel Hon. H. R. L. G. Alexander, D.S.O., M.C.	1928	1930
Colonel R. V. Pollok, C.B.E., D.S.O.	1930	

Commanding Officers 1*st Bn. Irish Guards :*

Lt.-Col. R. J. Cooper, M.V.O.	1900—1904
Lt.-Col. D. J. Proby	1904—1908
*Lt.-Col. G. C. Nugent, M.V.O.	1908—1909 Killed in Action.
†Lt.-Col. C. Fitz Clarence, V.C.	1909—1913 Killed in Action.
Lt.-Col. Hon. G. H. Morris	1913—1914 Killed in Action 1.9.1914

Commanding Officers of 1*st Bn. during the Great War :*

Major H. H. Stepney ..	2.9.1914—17.9.1914 Killed in Action.
*Lt.-Col. Lord Ardee, C.B., C.B.E.	18.9.1914—3.11.1914
‡Lt.-Col. (Temp.) Hon. J. F. Trefusis, D.S.O.	4.11.1914—15.8.1915 Killed in Action.
Lt.-Col. (Temp.) G. H. C. Madden	16.8.1915—1.11.1915 Killed in Action.
Lt.-Col. R. C. A. McCalmont, D.S.O.	2.11.1915— 2.3.1917

* The present Earl of Meath.

Lt.-Col. (Actg.) Hon. H. R. Alexander, D.S.O., M.C. ..	3.3.1917—23.5.1917
Lt.-Col. (Actg.) C. E. Rocke, D.S.O.	24.5.1917—11.7.1917
Lt.-Col. (Actg.) R. V. Pollok, C.B.E., D.S.O.	12.7.1917—19.6.1918
Lt.-Col. (Actg.) R. R. C. Baggallay, D.S.O., M.C. ..	20.6.1918 to return to England.

Commanding Officers of 2nd Bn. during Great War from August 16th, 1915 *:*

Lt.-Col. Hon. L. J. P. Butler, C.M.G., D.S.O.	16.8.1915— 5.5.1916
Lt.-Col. P. L. Reid, O.B.E. ..	12.5.1916—12.1.1917
Lt.-Col. E. B. Greer, M.C. ..	13.1.1917—31.7.1917 Killed in Action.
Major R. H. Ferguson ..	1.8.1917—1.10.1917
Lt.-Col. (Actg.) Hon. H. R. Alexander, D.S.O., M.C.	2.10.1917—3.11.1918
Lt.-Col. (Actg.) A. F. L. Gordon, D.S.O., M.C. ..	6.11.1918 to return to England.

Commanding Officers 1st Bn. since the Great War :

Lt.-Col. Hon. T. E. Vesey ..	1918—1922
Lt.-Col. Hon. H. R. Alexander, D.S.O., M.C.	1922—1926
Lt.-Col. R. V. Pollok, C.B.E., D.S.O.	1926—1930
Lt.-Col. Viscount Gough, M.C.	1930

* Colonel Nugent (Temp. Brig.-Gen.) was killed on 31.5.1915 while in command of 5th London Infantry Brigade.

† Colonel FitzClarence (Temp. Brig.-Gen.) was killed on 12.11.1914 while in command of the 1st Guards Brigade.

‡ Lt.-Col. Hon. J. F. Trefusis (Temp. Brig.-Gen.) was killed on 24.10.1915 while in command of 20th Infantry Brigade.

APPENDIX E.

THE VICTORIA CROSS.

The Regiment had three Victoria Crosses in the Great War. They were awarded to L/Cpl. M. O'Leary, L/Sgt. T. Moyney and Guardsman T. Woodcock.

Below is given the account from the Gazette of how each won the Victoria Cross.

No. 3556 L/Cpl. Michael O'Leary, 1st Bn. Irish Guards.

For conspicuous bravery at Cuinchy on the 1st February, 1916. When forming one of the storming party which advanced against the enemy's barricades he rushed to the front and himself killed five Germans who were holding the first barricade, after which he attacked a second barricade, about 60 yards further on, which he captured, after killing three of the enemy and making prisoners of two more.

" L/Cpl. O'Leary thus practically captured the enemy's position by himself, and prevented the rest of the attacking party from being fired on."

L/Cpl. O'Leary was subsequently promoted to Sergeant, and was later appointed to a commission in the Connaught Rangers.

No. 7708 L/Sgt. John Moyney, 1st Bn. Irish Guards.

" For most conspicuous bravery when in command of fifteen men forming two advanced posts. In spite of being surrounded by the enemy he held his posts for ninety-six hours, having no water and little food. On the morning of the fifth day a large force of the enemy advanced to dislodge him. He ordered his men out of their shell-holes, and, taking the initiative, attacked the advancing enemy with bombs, while he used his Lewis Guns with great effect from the flank. Finding himself surrounded by superior numbers, he led back his men in a charge through the enemy, and reached a stream which lay between the posts and the line. Here he instructed his men to cross at once while he and Pte. Woodcock remained to cover the retirement.

"When the whole of his force had gained the south-west bank unscathed he himself crossed under a shower of bombs. It was due to endurance, skill and devotion to duty shown by this N.C.O. that he was able to bring his entire force safely out of action."

No. 8387 Pte. Thomas Woodcock, Irish Guards.

"For most conspicuous bravery and determination. He was one of the post commanded by L/Sgt. Moyney which was surrounded. The post held out for 96 hours, but after that time was attacked from all sides in overwhelming numbers and was forced to retire.

"Pte. Woodcock covered the retirement with a Lewis gun, and only retired when the enemy had moved round and up to his post and were only a few yards away. He then crossed the river, but hearing cries of help behind him, returned and waded into the stream amid a shower of bombs from the enemy and rescued another member of the party. The latter he carried across the open ground in broad daylight towards our front line, regardless of machine gun fire that was opened on him."

Pte. Woodcock was killed in action on March 27th, 1918.

Lieutenant (Acting Lieut.-Col.) J. N. Marshall, late Irish Guards, Special Reserve, was awarded the Victoria Cross while serving with the 16th Battalion Lancashire Fusiliers.

APPENDIX F.

ATHLETICS & BOXING EVENTS

which the Irish Guards have won since the War.

1919.

Won Lawson Cup.
Won Prince of Wales Challenge Cup.
D/Sgt. Murphy won Army Long Jump Championship.

1920.

Won Lawson Cup.
Won Prince of Wales Challenge Cup.
Sergeant Nolan won Army 440 yards Championship.
Battalion won Army Relay Race.

1921.

Won Aldershot Command Cross-Country Challenge Shield.

Won Aldershot Command Cross-Country Championship.

Won Relay Race and Tug-of-War events at Aldershot Command (130 st.) Athletic Championships.

Won Lawson Cup.
Won Prince of Wales Challenge Cup.

1922.

Proceeded to Constantinople.

1923.

1st Guards Brigade Sports (Constantinople):

Won Inter-Unit Cup.

Colonel Alexander won the Brigade One Mile Championship.

1924.

Won Lawson Cup.
Won Prince of Wales Challenge Cup.

1925.

Won Household Brigade Boxing Championships (Team)

Won London District Cross-Country Championship.
Won Lawson Cup.

1926.

Won Household Brigade Boxing Championship (Team).

Won Lawson Cup.

Won Prince of Wales Challenge Cup.

Won Aldershot Command Athletic Championship (Team).

1927.

Won Household Brigade Boxing Championships.

Won Dewar Trophy (Machine Gun).

1928.

Won Household Brigade Boxing Championships (Team).

1929.

Won Household Brigade Boxing Championships (Team).

Officers won Connaught Cup.

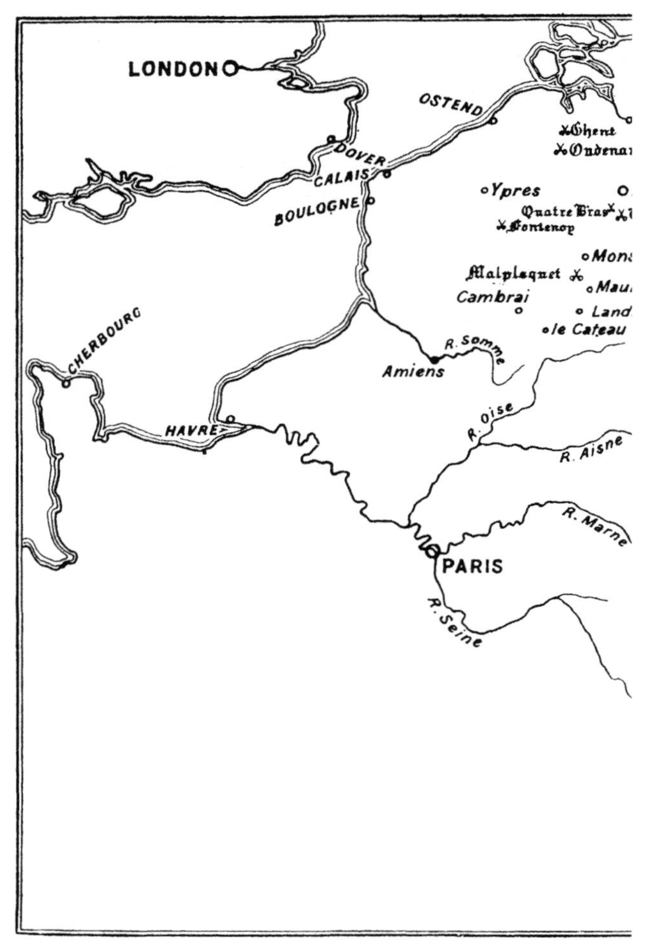

Sketch Map to illustrate the chief battles of
and the battles of

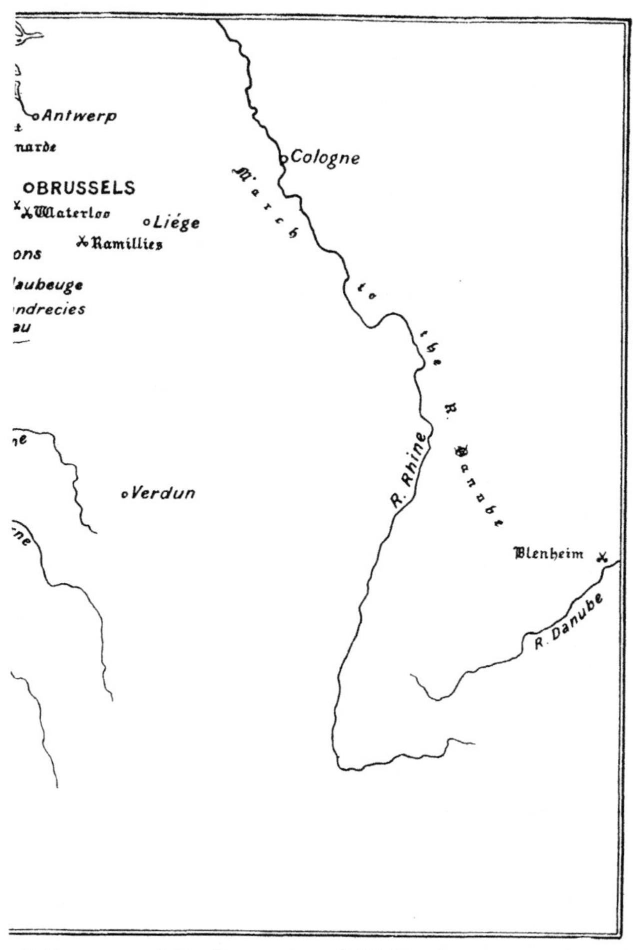

of the wars of Marlborough and Wellington,
of the Great War.

Printed and bound by Antony Rowe Ltd,
Eastbourne

Printed in Great Britain
by Amazon